MW00619184

Well, Hi There!

Engaging Stories to Stimulate Personal Growth

Well, Hi There!

Engaging Stories to Stimulate Personal Growth

by
Margaret Malone Faciszewski

Beloved, let us love one another…for God is love.

1John 4:7-8

Well, Hi There!
Engaging Stories to Stimulate Personal Growth

Copyright © 2005 by Margaret Malone Faciszewski
First Printing

All rights reserved. No part of this book may be reproduced in any form or by any electronic or mechanical means including information storage and retrieval systems without permission in writing from the publisher, except by a reviewer, who may quote brief passages in a review.

ISBN: 0-9767209-0-6
Excerpts from *Words of Wisdom* © 1993 and *Mother Teresa in My Own Words* © 1996 used with permission.

Library of Congress Control Number: 2005903332

Edited by Martha King, Notre Dame Sister Anita Rolenc, and Betty Jean Herrick

Cover and book design by M. Lambuth

Photographs copyright © Margaret Malone Faciszewski
Mountain scene photographed near Ouray, Colorado
Blooming rose photographed in Denver Botanic Gardens

Design & printing coordinated by:
Mary Beth Lambuth, Account Executive/Manager
Visual Images, Incorporated
1626 Franklin Street
Denver, Colorado 80218
303.388.5366

Printed in the United States of America

DEDICATION

To my beloved sons –
Thomas Gerard, Stephen Paul, and Edward Joseph –
who continue to amaze me with their
personal growth experiences, international relationships,
and multiple philanthropic contributions to society.
I love them dearly.

"If your heart is in the right place,
it affords you appropriate opportunity
to do things for others, to express your good will,
to let yourself go sentimentally, philanthropically."
B. C. Forbes (1880-1954)

FOREWORD

Socrates suggested that the unreflective life is not worth living. There is no evidence that Socrates meant this literally, but as a provocative statement to stimulate our thoughts and jar us out of passivity. Socrates realized that it is in the process of reflection that we integrate the disparate activities, emotions, and experiences of our daily lives and become more whole human beings. Reflection opens us to see the ordinary anew, to experience the sacred in the nitty-gritty of our lives. Reflection is the key to life-long learning. Margaret Malone Faciszewski's book, *Well, Hi There: Engaging Stories to Stimulate Personal Growth,* flows from these convictions. It is not a book to be studied or raced through, but a book to be enjoyed. A story a night provides food for thought in a manageable dose.

Faciszewski talks about family, extended and close; ancestors and grand-children; friends; and spirituality and education. The concrete details are replete from a goose hunting trip to fences and corrals, from immigrants to the Kansas prairie. Images come from such disparate settings as a bar mitzvah, a snowstorm in Texas, and sewing circles. The stories are of everyday life. Faciszewski captures our imaginations in her vignettes and triggers the memory of similar human experiences from our lives. The details of our lives are different, but she touches the cord of humanity that we all share: experiences of loss, anger, love, joy, guilt, and forgiveness.

Each story concludes with a provocative question or two to stimulate one's own reflection. Her direct and honest style creates a "safe space" for the reader to examine her or his own life with the same gentle honesty. Faciszewski's style reflects her personal belief that spiritual growth belongs not only to cloistered religious and monks, but to us common folks as well. God is here in the ordinary, if we but had eyes to see.

Diane Steele, S.C.L., Ph.D.
President
University of Saint Mary
Leavenworth, Kansas

CONTENTS

ACKNOWLEDGEMENTS

Impregnated with an idea for this book, I engaged the assistance of numerous people and resources. Many midwives – used here as a unisex term – supported the birthing process. They witnessed my groans, fatigue, and cries for help. I am grateful for their encouragement, support, and valuable suggestions. It is from these people that I drew my strength. Together, we rejoice in the successful, joyous birth of this writing project.

Generous thanks are in order for Diane Steele, SCL, who took time from her busy schedule as President of the University of Saint Mary to write the foreword for this book. Her knowledge, wisdom, talent, and energy are assets to all.

Carl Unrein, President and CEO of the Saint Joseph Hospital Foundation, and Dave Partheymuller, President of The Normandy Group, deserve major thanks for their time in reading the manuscript and writing reviews for the back cover. They are exceptional gentlemen of kindness and integrity.

I am also indebted to Mary Beth Lambuth, Account Executive/Manager of Visual Images, who coordinated the book design and printing process. She is a talented businesswoman with gracious communication skills and bountiful creative energy.

Proofreader and inspiring friend, Martha King, enthusiastically edited each story with skill and insight. Notre Dame Sister Anita Rolenc, a veteran English teacher, edited the manuscript and offered valuable suggestions. Alumni friend, Betty Jean Herrick, an avid reader and skilled writer, also edited the manuscript, noting important literary observations. My sincere thanks to these three persons who assisted in the final "polishing" of the writing project.

I am grateful to the staff at Marycrest Retreat Center and Mother Cabrini Shrine who offered me space for writing and editing. These quiet areas provided peaceful settings for the creative spirit to flow freely.

While the following list is not all-inclusive, it remains an attempt to show my gratitude to many family members and friends who became a part of this project: Mary Alice Bramming, Sister Mary Cecilia Carig, Mary Malone Cummings, Sister LaVonne Guidoni, Sister Marie Paula Hardy, Jim Malone, Ian Pearson, Sister Mary Joy Peter, Joel Phillips, Lindsay Smith, Kathleen Stark, Sonya Unrein, Sister Kathleen Waterman, Stephanie Zingg, and Pete, my faithful traveling companion.

Posthumously, I thank my beloved parents for giving me life, basic values and beliefs, six siblings, and unforgettable life experiences. Their love, care, and familial devotion provided the basis for many stories.

In advance, I offer my gratitude to "agents" who promote the sale of *Well, Hi There*. Through their efforts, many charitable organizations will benefit from the book proceeds. By working collectively to help those in need, we will enhance the quality of life for other human beings.

PROLOGUE

Long before I transitioned from my job as a school counselor, I decided I wanted to write a book. In teaching Career Awareness, one of the general guidelines shared was that statistically a significant number of people experience four careers in a lifetime. It is comforting to know that after years as a teacher, homemaker, and counselor, I now – with my fourth career as an author – fit into the world-of-work mold.

Somewhere along the path of reading and listening to audiobooks, I recall the statement, "An author does not choose the book, but rather the book chooses its author." In my case, I believe the statement to be true. Interesting and challenging personal experiences within the pie chart of spiritual, familial, career, and community areas guided the creation of this story collection. My intention in sharing these writings is to assist other people with their life-long learning process.

In facilitating workshops as well as addressing audiences as a keynote speaker, I realized the need for the written word to supplement my materials. Experience has shown that when people become engaged in a topic, they are more likely to encounter active learning – especially when leaving a session with useful information, the support of others in attendance, and a plan for growth and success.

Each short story included in this book relates, in part, to an event, person, experience, or idea from my life. The exercises after each story may be used in a variety of ways: addressing individual responses through writing, art mediums, music, verbal interaction, contemplative arts, drama, dance, or other venues of personal interest. As with any book, readers will gain varying levels of enjoyment and learning in processing its contents. I highly encourage following through with the designed learning opportunities in order to individualize each story and thereby experience growth. Readers may not agree with factions of particular short stories. In challenging the author's perspective, additional personal growth may take place.

Technically, the book is a combination of fact and fiction, and thus evolves into an eclectic bit of prose. Recorded quotations are not exact, but as I recall them to have been spoken. Fictitious names have been used to protect individual privacy. The core Malone family takes on the imaginary *O'Neill* surname. Truth is, renaming people and locations elicited creativity, and it became an engaging game of sorts to select the appropriate name for each person and place.

I trust that you will enjoy these stories, consider your own life journey, and become a more actualized person for giving time to the process.

Margaret Malone Faciszewski

Part I

GROWING UP INNOCENT

(Family)

"Life without love is like a tree without blossom and fruit."

Kablil Gibran (1883-1931)

A One-Horse Open Sleigh

Over a half century ago, my father borrowed a genuine one-horse open sleigh from a friendly neighbor. Vividly, as if it were happening this moment, I remember the bitterly cold moonlit night when my siblings, our mother, and I huddled together in the open sleigh, covered with numerous blankets. Dad, on the other hand, sat toward the front, next to the driver who skillfully led the horse. It was Christmas Eve. By singing carols through chattering teeth for the entire one-and-a-half mile journey, we prepared ourselves for midnight Mass being held at a mission church. Although a short distance, the blanket-covered horse labored hard as he pulled our large family to church that starry night, then dutifully waited for us while we attended the celebration of Christ's birth.

Such a glorious night for observing the universe's brilliant stars and a bright, full moon. Looking downward, one saw glistening snow, so crisp from subzero temperatures. The sounds of horse hooves' clickety-clack-clack on the snowpacked road and the driver's periodic snap of the reins created musical accompaniment to the caroling. Riding in the one-horse open sleigh with my family many Christmas seasons ago, I recall the comfort, security, and love provided by being snuggled together as a family on such a joyful night.

All families cannot create such storybook celebrations for their special occasions. Yet each can make its own memories through picnics, family dinners, activities, trips together, reunions – just to name a few. Basically, family connectedness is a matter of spending relaxed time together – to be present, chatty, or quiet; to laugh, to play, to pray; to celebrate the unique gifts of each family member.

Gratefully, I acknowledge my parents for providing family activities such as birthday dinners, chess games, sing-a-longs, summer picnics, and rides in a one-horse open sleigh. In their humble, non-pretentious manner, Mom and Dad presented lifetime gifts of cherished family memories.

Describe a special growing-up memory.

What can you do to recapture a similar joy in your present world?

Everyone Needs a Hobby

In her wisdom, my mother often remarked that everyone needed a hobby – an interest to sharpen the mind, soothe the soul, and bring relaxation into one's life. She herself became skilled at many hobbies: sewing, embroidery, knitting, crocheting, leatherwork, gardening, quilting, and ceramics. Rearing seven children and laboring daily as she managed the household, she regularly made time to explore her interests, thus creating many heirlooms that became part of her legacy.

"Hobbies," Mother stated, "get you through the tough times." And difficult times she certainly experienced as she lived through the Depression, harsh Dakota winters, and hot dry summers. Several illnesses, the loss of a child as well as beloved family members, and crippling arthritis caused her much emotional and physical pain. Nevertheless, she reached out to help others. Being awarded South Dakota's coveted Eminent Homemaker of the Year award, she exemplified her true pioneering spirit as a community contributor.

During the final years of her life, she remained at home with the assistance of twenty-four-seven care. It was during this time that she began her final project, the crocheted dish mats. Prior to this last year of illness, she purchased a crocheted dish mat at a craft fair. The new pattern fascinated her inquisitive mind. Temporarily, it was set aside, then brought forth when she desired a challenge to occupy her mind as she dealt with arthritic aches and pains, in addition to a newly diagnosed terminal illness.

For two months, Mother studied the pattern, attempting with crochet hook and yarn, to recreate the design. At last, she determined that the original dish mat had been crocheted by a left-handed person, resulting in a reverse direction of stitches! In the next two months, she reversed each stitch pattern in her mind and recorded the directions, thereby creating *her* original dish mat with determination, ancestral stubbornness, and tenacity. Next, she set a goal to make additional dish mats for her caregivers and family members. With various yarn hues and interesting color combinations, she proceeded with her mission, completing thirty-five items.

Recipients treasure these creative gifts, for they represent Mother's strength, her artistic talents, the determination to keep her hands and mind occupied as she dealt with getting her affairs in order, struggled to walk with the aid of a walker, eat food prepared and served to her, and sleep intermittently after being tucked into bed. Following her own advice, having hobbies served her well in living her life journey, and in managing the mysterious, never before ventured, dying process.

Describe a person in your life who has found a healthy strategy for dealing with life or near-death issues.

Tell about a hobby that challenges your mind, body, and spirit.

I Made It!

Many times we survive challenging experiences and then exuberantly shout, "I made it!" Arguably, within each year, people of all ages echo this exclamation with relief and joy – like a pre-school child finishing her final year and then being promoted to kindergarten; a senior graduating from high school; or a marathon runner crossing the finish line.

This same feeling of accomplishment overwhelmed my spirit the day I survived five years of my spouse's retirement. Why such a glorious relief – accomplishment, if you will? Well, you see, some twenty years ago I spent a week with my mother and father, as had been my tradition for a number of summers. While visiting and helping them with household chores, my mother presented me with curious predictions of my future.

"Just wait until your husband retires. Then, your troubles will *really* begin," she lamented. Puzzled, I wondered, *Could this period of life's journey be so painstakingly challenging?* To add to this mysterious foretelling, like a fortune-teller looking into her crystal globe, Mother told me a story about my paternal grandparents.

"Your grandfather," she said, "was a domineering man. His wife, your grandmother, dreaded his retirement and told me she wouldn't live long after he quit working. To assist her with this traumatic period of her life," Mom continued, "your grandmother devoted time to charitable works. Nevertheless, she died, as predicted, within five years after Grandpa's retirement."

In recent years, this story became more realistic, haunting me as I, too, considered whether or not I would experience the same fate. Often, I pondered:

Had my grandmother, the woman after whom I had been named, laid the cobblestone path for my journey?

When the five-year anniversary of my spouse's retirement passed, I drew a joyous sigh of relief, and happily felt permission to continue creating my own life experiences. Like the pre-schooler, the high school senior, and marathon runner, I jubilantly stated, "I made it!" Now, like a cancer survivor who has been given a second chance at life, I eagerly look forward to setting new goals and traveling life's journey with a renewed spirit of freedom, adventure, and enthusiasm.

Consider a personal prediction shared with you.

How did it affect your life?

It's All His Fault

Blaming comes naturally to a child, a trait that one hopefully outgrows with maturity. This I know to be true because it happened in a situation involving my brother John, the one commissioned as my protector and placed in charge of me as I walked to and from school each day. He was a quiet young man, but totally responsible, taking his assignment of guarding me – notably given to him by our mother – very seriously. In so doing, *he* became the reason for my last spanking. It was all his fault!

Memory recalls that when I was in fourth or fifth grade, one of my friends invited me to come home with her after school. This was to be quite a treat as there were not too many children to play with in our tiny town, so I desperately wanted to accept her invitation. Doing so, however, meant walking two miles over hills and down valleys to her house, then returning home by myself, all without the permission of either my brother or my mother. *But, how could I resist?* I thought. *It would be so fun to play at someone else's house for a change*. Using elementary logic, I made the decision to join my friend, hoping that there would not be ill consequences.

Arriving home about two hours late after the end of the school day, my mother met me anxiously at the door. She sternly asked, "Where have you been?"

"Oh," I replied, "I had to stay after school."

Wisely, she made no further response. However, within the next twenty-four hours she checked my story with the school officials only to find – you guessed it – that I did not stay after school for any reason. What came next resulted in

Mom's punishment of a "good talking to" and a stinging spanking. Oh, that hurt! For days, I angrily ignored my brother-protector who failed to stick up for me. Since he chose not to align himself with my story, I believed it was his entire fault that I got punished.

Perhaps this experience was the beginning of one of life's most important lessons. Living the journey is about choices, making decisions, and accepting responsibility for our actions and their ensuing consequences. It's simple, really – this living life. But, why does it take so long to learn the art of discernment, and to realize that each decision we make has an effect, albeit some more longer lasting, more positive or negative, than others? Taking time to collect data as well as weigh pros and cons of choices assist individuals in walking through life as people of integrity, kindness, and compassion.

Guiding children gives parents the opportunity and responsibility to instill values and beliefs in their youngsters, while also teaching them to be responsible, independent citizens. Allowing adult children to follow their own choices-decisions-consequences-responsibility formula (CDCR) may be one of the most difficult challenges of parenthood. But once jettisoned into adulthood, offspring are responsible for their own choices. Decisions about marriage, divorce, religious affiliation, children, careers, and areas in which to live all become their responsibility. On the other hand, as parents of adult children, we pray – until our dying breath – that our children will be graced with the ability to make wise choices, while we remain available and supportive to them when they seek our knowledge, wisdom, and guidance.

With wisdom gained in living some eighty years, my mother referred to children and grandchildren when she said, "I'm just not going to worry about them any more. Someday, they'll get it (life) all figured out!" Following her wise decision may be worthy of note for all parents.

Ultimately, people do not have the right to design someone else's journey. Yet we can nurture, listen, and love one another as well as accept others as they are and not as we would like them to be. Living one's choices, then, becomes not an "It's all his fault!" situation, but an opportunity for growth, change, and wisdom.

Describe someone in your lifetime that you blamed for a particular incident.

In honest reflection, what did that incident teach you?

It's Snowing!

Miraculously, the sound of another person melodically saying, "It's snowing!" has an air of magic about it – like a lame person walking once again; a toddler speaking his first word; or a baby robin attempting an initial flight from the nest. On several occasions, which I will forever hold dear in my memory, I heard this statement surrounding a snowy event, and felt its mystery, its magic.

One April 30th, it became necessary to make a late night telephone call. Having received news of my father's death, I offered to pass this sorrowful message on to my brother as quickly as possible. I dialed Gene's number, expecting to hear his voice. Surprisingly, his daughter Laura greeted me with a hesitating, "Hello" – a normal, cautious response when answering a middle-of-the-night call. Perhaps she wanted to shield her parents from alarming news. At any rate, when I shared the urgent message, she paused. Although unable to observe Laura's reaction or action, I envisioned that in those moments of quiet, she peaked out the window, for she responded by saying, "It's snowing!" The tone of her voice indicted to me that she realized a mysterious event had just taken place. Her paternal grandfather had transitioned into eternity, and he was sending his pure love to us through the freshly falling snowflakes. Heavenly peace enhanced that moment of awesome beauty.

On another occasion, this time toward the end of May, we had just moved into a new house. After months of sorting through household items, packing boxes until our fingers became callused, then unpacking until the wee hours of the morning, we felt exhausted! It comes as no surprise, then, that we fell into a deep sleep each night of that first week. After seven days of assisting with the moving process, our son prepared to return to his own home and career obligations. Leaving very early on that late May morning, he tiptoed into our bedroom to tell us good-bye. In so doing, he momentarily glanced out our yet-uncurtained window, and exclaimed, "It's snowing!" A present had arrived: a gift of hope, of new beginnings, comfortable tomorrows.

While the first two incidents occurred in Colorado, the next scenario took place in Texas while I was caring for grandchildren. Naturally, this area doesn't have the type of winters experienced in northern states. However, on initial onset of this March stay with four small children, the weather turned quite cold, with blustery winds howling during the night. At the crack of dawn, the seven-year-old jumped out of bed, peaked through the venetian blinds, and shrieked, "It's snowing!" What excitement transformed the sleeping household! Immediately the children wanted to go outside and play in the three inches of snow that was such an unusual treat for them, like licking an ice cream cone or savoring a morsel of Swiss chocolate for the very first time.

These three life experiences illustrate that "It's snowing!" is a statement unto itself. For every falling snowflake is a miracle, with each design uniquely different from the other. Yes, when it snows, this gem-like gift from Mother Nature evolves into a mysterious, magic show for earth's inhabitants.

Tell about a "mysterious, magical" statement or event you experienced.

What meaning does it have for your life?

My Way, My Time

Finally, I am able to let go of guilt generated five years past. For only yesterday I learned, through an enlightening session facilitated by an experienced Hospice nurse, that many patients choose approximately when they are going to die. Also, based on her observations of the dying, she contends that people do not die alone. She added that many parents, especially, die without their children surrounding them. She explained that, with spirits hovering nearby, the dying have "others" with them. How I wish I had known and, as time allowed, accepted these facts after my mother died. Perhaps then my heart would have felt *peace,* most notably around the anniversary of her death, and *comfort* that she, as was her right, chose the approximate manner and timing of her death.

With experience, knowledge, and kindness, Mother's doctor daily met with her in her final two-week hospital stay of her life. Together, they talked about a blood transfusion – which she refused; they reviewed the resuscitation option – which she declined. What did she want? Her desire included returning to her private home, and not checking into the Old Folks Home, as she coined the local nursing home.

Learning that returning home was not a viable option, I believe Mother set into motion the final stages of the dying process. She ate and drank minimally – much to the nurses', family's, and friends' frustration and chagrin. She conversed only when necessary, slept a lot, although intermittently. The compassionate parish priest visited her several times for prayerful comfort.

As I sat with her the day before her transition into eternal life, Mother awakened and focused her eyes on the wall calendar hanging near the foot of her bed.

"What day is it?" she asked.

"Friday," I replied.

She then closed her eyes, continuing to sleep. The significance of this event is the fact that her four sons were still on their annual Nebraska goose-hunting safari. Traditionally it ended on Saturday. I am convinced that she did not want her premature death to interfere with their hunting excursion. Consequently, she drew her last breath Saturday afternoon.

Why have I carried five years of guilt about my mother's final earthly moments? Actually, it lies in the fact that she died alone (or so I believed). Unaware that she was in her final hours of life, I ate a quick lunch with family members. Returning to the hospital, I witnessed the nurse hurriedly walking down the hall. "She just slipped away. She simply went to sleep," she said. *Oh my God.* I thought, *I was only a minute or two late. I wasn't there for her as she drew her last breath!* The wise nurse gently tried to explain that dying alone, with no one nearby, occurs frequently. But I couldn't accept this happening to *my* mother.

In reflection, I believe Mother – being an independent, personally private woman – chose not to have any of her living children near her bedside for her final transition. To a reasonable degree, she controlled her life, and then her dying. Now, I understand and am comforted in knowing that she *didn't* die alone, but surrounded by her Lord and the spirits of predeceased family and friends.

My mother made decisions about her final life-care and estimated the day she would die. Likewise, she escaped living at the Old Folks Home. Ah, yes, my ninety-four-year-old mother was determined that her passing be "My Way, My Time."

Describe a loss event (death, divorce, move, or other traumatic experience).

What did you learn that helped you move forward with your life?

Playing Catch with Dad

Sometimes I pose the question: How many dads play catch with their daughters? Most assuredly, I enthusiastically and proudly claim, "Mine did!" Many evenings after dinner, my Dad would ask, "Want to play some catch?"

Excitedly, I always said, "Yes!" Together, we would fetch baseball and mitts, walk down the backporch stairs, and proceed to the side yard – the one with the windmill trimmed with grapevines, the swing, and vegetable garden. And, oh, the potato cellar that harbored gigantic (at least from a young child's perspective) black spiders staring at me from their webs.

Yet in this side yard was room for two energetic ball players. Back and forth the ball sailed, the players smiling, laughing, and chatting. I don't remember the conversation topics. They weren't important. Active togetherness was the key element fostering memories of *joy,* feeling special, and valuable bonding.

Now, I wonder, *where does one seek those contagiously happy moments of youth? In the service of others? In nature? In contemplation with God? In gatherings with family and friends? Where does one capture the essence of innocent, unadulterated, free-spirited happiness?* Ah, finding answers to these questions is a goal for which one ought to aim.

On this glorious spring day, I am pausing on a well-worn bench near a small pond at the city's botanic gardens. Nearby, two large Canadian geese are resting peacefully with heads tucked under their wings. Sleeping on the wooden deck two feet in front of me, they, unknowingly, bring child-like joy into my heart, like that same authentic peace and happiness felt while playing catch with Dad.

Another moment of joy occurred as I strolled along a quiet Florida beach.

Finding intact sand dollars brought delight to my heart. Continuing my walk, I looked up from the beach and focused on the ocean waves. Twenty feet from the shore, I noticed a school of dolphins, gracefully swimming in the same direction that I walked. For me, the experience constituted the same pleasure that I imagine is felt by people who swim with the dolphins. It felt like recreating with friends, enjoying an activity together in Mother Nature's wonderland. An awesome experience!

These scenes remind me that frequently we are provided opportunities for energizing periods of rejuvenation. Pausing to encircle them into our lives, opening our arms to the experiences, and enfolding the precious moments into our hearts, we will feel the peace and joy intended by the Creator of the Universe.

Recall an occasion of pure delight.

Where, how, and when can you recapture this peaceful joy
in your everyday life?

The General Store

Growing up next to a store presented numerous opportunities to learn strategies for living life as an independent adult. This general store owned by my parents provided initial on-the-job training, lessons in teamwork, and positive customer relationship practices. In addition, it fostered the establishment of critical values, hopes, and dreams for the future.

Neatly and compactly organized, the store offered almost everything from soup to bolts. I know, because every New Year's Day my six siblings and I counted every single item! While Mother prepared our holiday meal, we spent the entire day in the store with our dad and Uncle Mike counting...and counting... and counting. Being assigned to the hardware section, my four brothers set about sorting through nuts, bolts, screws, wire, rope, and tools. My two sisters and I, given the dry goods area, proceeded to list numbers of: yards on each fabric bolt; spools of thread; embroidery floss; containers of glass beads used for Native American beadwork; socks and hosiery; crochet thread and yarn; mittens and gloves; blouses, dresses, sweaters, shawls, and shirts.

When "the boys" or "the girls" finished their assigned areas, they proceeded to the sections of cowboy boots, shoes, and snowboots; the basic food items of canned goods, fresh meat, cereals, and dried fruits; and standard baking ingredients. *How,* I wonder, *did we count pickled pigs feet and horseradish in large jar containers, bulk dried beans in deep drawers, bins of unshelled peanuts, large boxes of candy and bubble gum, sacks of Bull Durham tobacco, and gallons of gasoline and kerosene?* Indeed, this inventory task taught my siblings and me important lessons in accountability, the value of each item, tenacity, stick-to-it-ive-ness, and teamwork.

Without the need of an interview or resume, Dad gave us our first paying job. Sweeping out the store after each business day, when I was five or six years old, became an opportunity for me to learn the value of a dime. I say *dime* because that is exactly what I remember being paid.

My first incentive to earn a dime sat atop a high glass showcase holding a sampling of dresses and blouses. She was a beautiful doll all dressed in pink that I unhesitatingly named "Geraldine." She rested there as part of a raffle to raise money for our elementary school. Each ticket cost ten cents, one lone dime. For weeks, I asked my dad, "May I sweep the store floor this evening?"

Smiling, for he understood my incentive, he replied, "Sure."

I spent months wishing, hoping, and working with the intense desire to win Geraldine. Finally, the raffle date arrived. With eager anticipation, I watched and prayed as the delegated person pulled out the winning ticket. Hearing my name called brought tears of joy on one of the happiest days of my childhood.

As we matured in age, we were given responsibility of waiting on customers, using the cash register, noting credit purchases, pumping gasoline, and listing checks at the end of the day. On one occasion, Dad gave one of my four brothers the task of paying necessary bills. With due diligence, Roy proceeded to write *and* sign each check. Proudly, he presented the completed project to Dad. He carefully reviewed the stack of checks. As a patient father, he responded, "Roy, you only have authority to write out the date, business or person's name, and amount due. Signing the checks is performed by the person who has ample funds in the bank."

"Oh," said Roy, having just learned another life-long skill.

Living in this electronic age, I am curious as to whether or not my siblings pay their bills electronically, allow a software program to balance their checkbooks, or use an ATM machine. Regardless of their current practices, working in the family store and performing related tasks helped prepare us for adult lives as responsible homemakers, wage earners, citizens, and community servants in the present world.

Think about childhood experiences that taught you important values for responsible living.

How can you teach responsibility, the value of a dime, life-long skills, and accountability to children and young adults?

The Pies: A Mother's Message to Her Sons

I have been watching all the commotion that seems to go on in preparation for your yearly goose-hunting trip. What a site to observe from this heavenly location! However, I can't figure out why you neglected the pie request until two days before your trip departure this year. Could it be that you are beginning to think more wisely of your healthy hearts, your waistlines, the bakers' energy and stress? How did this tradition get started anyway? Was it due to your father's habit of taking fresh homemade pies with him when he went on his hunting outings?

I don't believe you will see many geese this year. I watch Meg as she walks around a city park, and sometimes hear her telling the geese to stay away from Nebraska. She tells them stories about grumpy old men that eat four different kinds of pie while they sit in the goose pit, listening for unsuspecting geese to find their decoys. She really admires the ability and nature of the geese to fly so far in formation, all the while watching out for one another. Honestly, I think she believes you should be learning lessons from these birds instead of eating pie, chasing skunks, and telling tall tales.

All year long I hear Meg advising you to plan ahead as well as to contact daughters, sons, nieces, and nephews about supplying your traditional apple, mince, cherry, and pumpkin pies. Let me give you a hint. Remember, whatever you do when making your special request of these gracious folks, do not use that four-letter word, *duty,* in reference to making pies for hunters!

I've come to the realization that you boys have the innate ability to be pretty good cooks. In fact, I believe that you could learn to make quite tasty pies.

Maybe one of these days you could bake one or two and surprise all the women in the family who succumb to your stories about not being able to provide your own desserts! Actually, you may learn, too, that feeding your stomachs with fat-laden fuel may not be in your best interest. But, I'm not going to worry about this situation for I know you'll get it all figured out one of these years.

We're all doing fine up here. Believe it or not, we are not far away from our earthly O'Neill family. Pretty nifty how we can get from place to place so quickly. Well, I need to go check on some family members on your planet who have been asking for guidance. Have a good time in the goose pit, but let the geese enjoy their time on earth, too.

Love you ~ Mother

Select a person who is no longer on earth. Place yourself in that person's spirit.

What messages would she or he have for your living style?

The Post Office

Today – which would have been my father's one hundred and tenth birthday – I have chosen to share a story that highlights his unconditional love, quick wit, and innocent use of Gerontology Psychology 101. In his easy-going, patient manner, he used a survival strategy with his aging father that exemplified humorous and effective solutions in dealing with the daily demands of caring for a sometimes challenging, dogmatic father.

My parents owned a general store, which also housed the small town's United States Post Office. In the mid-twentieth century, mail delivery arrived by a mailcarrier driving a pickup truck filled with collected letters and packages stuffed into mailsacks. Consequently, the outgoing mail needed to be safely tucked into these same sacks and securely locked. The organization of empty mailsacks, then, became the responsibility of my grandpa.

My paternal grandfather, Harry O'Neill, suffered from dementia, hearing loss, and poor eyesight, as well as the No Hobby Syndrome. Hence, he sat idle for hours, no longer able to read his beloved newspaper. In an effort to help him occupy an hour or so of his seemingly long day, Dad gave him the responsibility of folding and stacking the empty mailsacks and placing them in their designated area. Meticulously and deliberately – for that was the nature of this former railroad engineer – he folded each bag to perfection, placing the finished product in a neat pile. This morning chore normally consumed about one hour.

After lunch and a nap, my Grandpa Harry, who lived with my parents, frequently walked to the general store located less than a block from their home. Finding his son, he asked, "What can I do now?" Like a three-year old pestering his mom for activity suggestions, Grandpa relied on my father for entertainment and assigned chores.

Unbeknownst to Grandpa, however, my father, prior to this afternoon visit, had unfolded all the mailsacks and placed them in the to-be-folded location. In answer to Grandpa's question, Dad responded, "Well, the mailsacks need to be folded before the mailman's arrival tomorrow. Would you like to take care of them now?"

"Sure," Grandpa said. With his memory loss, he had no realization of performing double duty on this same assignment. Again, another hour – more or less – of his time occupied, he felt pleased that he had assisted his son with the postal duties.

Numerous times I have recalled this story of "The Post Office" for it continues to teach me about the importance of thinking creatively, treating elders with respect while helping them fill their long days, and laughing about challenges as we discover creative solutions to life's nuances and seemingly impossible situations.

Recall a situation in which you found yourself
creating a job for someone.

How did this endeavor work for you and the other person(s)?

The Red Floor

The old country house in which I grew up sheltered many folks from outdoor elements. Prior to my parents' purchase, it served as a resting place for cowboys, salesmen, and families traveling to their destinations. Throughout our growing up years, the house received many makeovers: painting, wallpapering, and the addition of a much-needed bathroom. Yet one constant remained – the red linoleum kitchen floor.

When I was a young child, I heard my mother once remark, "This linoleum is over thirty years old. *Golly,* I thought, *who'd ever keep something that long?* At that time, thirty years seemed an eternity. *So, that's why it took us so long to polish it,* I concluded. *It was old enough to be dead!*

The polishing, you see, became the personal chore for Charlie and me. Mom usually washed and applied paste wax to the floor during the day. After we arrived home from school and had a snack, we busied ourselves with before-dinner chores. Now, we had a certain technique to this important duty. With a big bath towel folded in a square and placed on the floor, I sat cross-legged atop the mound as Charlie pulled me around – all according to his self-designated speed and pattern. His temperament also determined how I found myself being pulled this way and that. If in a bad mood, or in one of his stubborn streaks, I had to hold on to Charlie's shirt so as not to fall off.

That's not all of the story. To test the floor's polishing job, we involved the family cat, Fluffy. Placing a chair in the doorway, the hurdle in place, we took the cat down the hallway, placed her four paws on the floor, turned her around several times, pointed her in the direction of the chair, and said, "Go!"

Fluffy scampered as fast as she could, jumped the wooden hurdle, landed on the floor, and slid across the room. The length of her skid became a test. No skid at all meant we had to do more polishing; a medium skid received a satisfactory cheer; a long skid received a loud, "Yea!"

In this same kitchen with the infamous red floor, my siblings and I took turns washing and drying dishes. No automatic dishwasher in our household! Using large embroidered tea towels, we dried each dish, or returned it to the soapy water if it didn't pass inspection. Sometimes, the dish washer couldn't keep up with those of us drying the dishes. In this downtime, periodically we held our towels by diagonal corners, twirled them around while stretching them tautly, and then proceeded to snap one another's legs.

"Ouch, that hurt!" the victim screamed. More quick snaps followed the painful cries, which, in reality, were pleas for parental help. Mother, in her sergeant major mode, begrudgingly left her comfortable chair in the living room and came marching into the kitchen, saying, "Now you kids cut it out!" And, cut it out we did, only to smile at one another as she headed back to her rocking chair and crocheting.

The kitchen floor also became the workspace for making butter, another designated chore for Charlie and me. The butter churn was filled with cream from cows milked by siblings (since we weren't old enough for that chore *yet)*. We carefully placed the container on the floor. To hold it steady, I sat on the towel-draped top while Charlie turned the crank until butter became visible. The whole chore would not have taken so long, if he weren't always clowning around, laughing, and giving me a hard time about sitting still!

The red linoleum floor supported all sizes of feet as my mother and siblings (usually the girls!) prepared enormous amounts of food. Some still-talked about favorites are Mom's homemade bread, pear butter, and chicken stew. Preparing this last delicacy involved a series of steps.

Since we raised our own chickens for consumption, the initial procedure required someone to snatch the chickens and cut off their.... Well, you know what has to be done before feathers are plucked, down singed, and the chickens cut up in preparation for cooking. One day, as we were in the final stages of "dressing down the chicken," Mom said to me, "Remember to save the oldest hen for stew because the meat is too tough to serve as a fried-up chicken. An old hen only becomes *tender* when it is made into a stew!"

Brother Roy, not being present, didn't hear Mom's advice. Hence, as an adult, he searches for the oldest hen in the grocery store, because, he says, "Mom always used an old hen for stew because it made A TASTY STEW." What my older brother hasn't realized yet is that any chicken will make a stew *taste* good; but an old hen only becomes *tender* as it is cooked for several hours. A misfortune, indeed, that Roy and his brothers didn't spend more time standing on that old red floor helping Mom cook! In so doing, they would have learned a lot of her culinary secrets.

Finally, if the red linoleum floor could speak, it might relay stories of silent periods of lost loved ones, especially after a premature sibling's death; birthday celebrations; wedding party gatherings; and holiday get-togethers.

Folks always liked to gather in our warm kitchen with the red floor. It was homey there.

Which room in your living space feels especially homey?

What stories could you tell about some of the room's features?

The Rusty Nail

On my early morning walk today, I – after strolling past swaying prairie grass, red plum trees, and a rustic crossover bridge – observed an equestrian site much different from that of my childhood. With brilliant white fences and barns, manicured paths and trot runs, the setting appeared as if painted by a Kentucky artist.

Much different is my memory of horse troughs, bins for feed, haystacks, open pastures, and groomed horses. Even rounding up the horses became an interesting technique to observe. In coaxing them to venture nearby, my brother held out a bucket of oats and called each horse's name. Then, when close enough, he placed a looped rope around the neck. Once he bridled and saddled his catch, one of my brothers rode near another horse, twirling his lasso around his head and strategically aiming it to encircle the long neck. Frequently practicing this roping technique, all my brothers became quite expert with their young cowboy skills.

One particular day, though, my brothers decided to put horseback riding aside, try a new sport, and attempt to ride the young calves kept in a corral next to the barn. Our parents, especially Dad, gave strict orders not to ride the calves, as the young animals might be harmed. Although usually obedient in following parental rules, the temptation to learn a new riding skill became too great.

Climbing over the fence and into the corral, Roy, John, and Charlie discussed which brother would make the first attempt. Once decided, they proceeded to take turns riding the calves, just like the rodeo cowboys. All went well until

Charlie, as he was straddling the calf and hanging on for dear life, rode a bit too close to the corral's wooden fence post, puncturing his arm on a rusty nail. Blood oozed everywhere.

Frightened, but not willing to tell our parents about the incident, they devised a plan. The first step was to wash the injury. Since they would not go into the house for fear of being punished, they fetched water from the horse trough! Wrapping the injured arm tightly with a handkerchief, they repeated the mantra, "Cowboys are tough! Cowboys are tough! Cowboys are tough!" Poor Charlie survived the incident without a tetanus shot or even a thorough cleansing with clean water and antiseptic. More importantly, our parents never learned of the incident until many years later. Narrowly, the amateur cowboys had escaped inevitable consequences for this disobedient act.

Later, as siblings experienced life-challenges and medical surgeries, the initial chant changed slightly. Now, brothers and sisters remind one another that, "O'Neills are tough!" Normally, the response brings a smile and a twinkle to the eye as they recall my brothers' attempt at becoming skilled calf riders.

Consider a childhood decision that went against your parents' wishes.

What learned lesson assists you with your adult journey?

The Tapestry

Oh, to be an artist, to sit by a stream painting a picture representing a family's character, focus, and interests; to study what makes a family unique from others. What colors, symbols, type of thread would be needed to depict the unit?

Ah, but being an artistically-challenged individual must not keep me from creating my family tapestry! Through the written word, I am determined to decipher our family that has evolved from years of caring, sharing, and traveling the journey together. With completed manuscript in hand, I will seek a talented artist to design the family tapestry and a craftsperson to create the heirloom wall hanging.

To foster on-going bonding and strength of the family unit, I – since the arrival of the first grandchild – made a concerted effort to care for the children at least once a year so that their parents could escape out of town for several days. Being a long distance grandparent, these trips have given me multiple opportunities for establishing a relationship with the grandchildren. While not able to spend special occasions together, our family learned early on to believe that every day we are together is a day to be enjoyed in the holiday spirit of joy, peace, and love.

Mind you, these annual visits have not been without their special challenges. One winter trip to Minnesota will be remembered forever. Falling snow, covering an inch of ice on the driveway, made caring for four children between the ages of one and five a bit wearisome. The youngest child was still in diapers and not yet crawling or walking, and the oldest attended kindergarten. Because it was quite cold, the majority of time we spent indoors playing games, making cookies, and reading stories. After several days of indoor activity, I promised them – as a treat to look forward to and a mental readjustment for me – an outing to the local McDonald's restaurant and play area. Planning ahead, I wrote down their food requests before bundling up all four children in winter clothing, and snatching the diaper bag, pacifier, favorite stuffed animals, and blankets. Imagine buckling into carseats two overstuffed toddlers (with winter jackets, snowpants, mittens, and boots), checking that the two older children were securely strapped into their car seats, and moving quickly to anxious voices chanting, "Hurry up, Grandma!"

Okay, ready to go. Nervously, I prayed that, as I inched out the icy driveway, I could stop before turning on to the street. Windshield wipers keeping snowflakes at bay, I drove the five miles at snail speed, arriving at the drive-up window with my list of requests. But, alas, the van window had frozen shut! Jumping out of the car, I frantically presented my list to the attendant who kindly filled the order while I waited in the vehicle with hungry children.

Finally, I parked the van, then gathered bundled-up baby and Happy Meals. Instructing the other three to watch for moving cars, we crossed the parking lot into the warm building. The children gobbled down their food, for eating was a prerequisite to racing around and going up and down tunnels as if working out for an upcoming field day. The young infant seemed content to watch the flurry of activity as she munched on left-behind food. I nurtured my nerves and tummy with a Big Mac, large bag of french fries, and any leftovers that baby did not want. Before leaving, the whole gang (including grandma) savored ice cream cones together. Later that night, as I collapsed into bed, I breathed wearily and sighed, "Mission accomplished!"

Another hair-raising incident occurred with the Wisconsin set of grandchildren when they were four, six, and eight years old. With children fed, bathed, and the two younger ones tucked into bed, I played cards with the eight-year-old grandson. Game after game we enjoyed! Momentarily, though, we heard a "beep...beep...beep" continue for a while. A foreign sound to us, we quizzically looked at one another and asked, "What's that? Where's that noise coming from?" With the responsibility for these children becoming more pronounced, I grew anxious. Our grandson asked, "Should we call the fire department?" Unable to concentrate on the card game, and this pressing question consuming my thoughts and conversation, I made the 911 call.

Within minutes, the red fire engine came roaring down the country-graveled driveway with sirens blaring and red lights flashing. Dressed in full uniform and carrying equipment ready for action, volunteer firefighters rushed inside and proceeded to investigate every inch of the two-story house and basement. Finding no cause for alarm – and considering our responses to their many questions – they deducted that the steady beeps came from a carbon monoxide detector with low batteries. Oh, my. All that drama and action because I wasn't familiar with the beep…beep…beep signals!

What did parents do upon their return home to children, animals, and work responsibility? Of course, I don't know what they said to one another out of my hearing range. I just gathered, from their shaking heads and looks of disbelief, that they found it amazing that their grandchild-caregiver didn't have a clue about the no-brainer sounds given off from the contemporary safety device!

What does relaying these stories have to do with the tapestry? Revisiting the incidents helped to solidify mentally the core values and beliefs of our nuclear family. As a group, the four families make up a "helping others" kind of unit. The focal symbol of the tapestry, therefore, needs to be two overlapping hands – a smaller one representing intuitive, caring support; and a larger hand representing protective, technical strength. The two hands might then be encircled with symbols of human beings, animals, and our planet. Thus, the family's common interest in philanthropy – the sharing of time, talent, and treasure – becomes the central theme for the total design.

With an artist's precision, illustrations of four different residences would depict the lifestyles of core families: a two-story centurion farm house surrounded by grazing sheep, llamas, and deer; a ranch-style city home with views of Puget Sound and the Olympic Mountains; a spacious two-story suburban home nestled in a forest of trees, buffalo grass, and wildflowers; and a small patio home with a welcome mat and wrought iron bench on the front porch. Above each unique living space would be angels to protect and guide the lives of family members, even on icy roads and in beeping houses.

Strategically designed in the tapestry would be symbols describing family interests: a love of the outdoors; sports like cycling, fitness walking, jogging, soccer, hiking, swimming, and skiing; exploration of crafts, design work, painting, writing, and music.

The weaver needs to use strong, royal fibers, depicting the strength of the total family unit, even though individual families live in various areas of the world. While not often physically together, our family's bond is energized through communicative tools of telephone, electronic messages, and old-fashioned postal mail, providing necessary glue for family cohesiveness.

Let's see. Caring hands, houses, angels, symbols of common interests, and strong fibers have been selected for the tapestry. If the designer requests ideas for color choices, I might suggest using family birthstone colors, subtle earth tones to blend in our interest in the great outdoors, and a rich burgundy background to represent both familial love and philanthropic care of global brethren.

This family tapestry *can* become an artistically created, delicately woven, and proudly displayed heirloom. Maybe someday the completed product will become a reality – a strategically placed wall hanging for my rocking chair days, helping to keep my long-distance family ever near.

Think about the core values and beliefs of your family.

What symbols, colors, and type of fiber would be used for your family tapestry?

The View Outside

I especially loved the two bedroom windows in my childhood home. Gracefully, they were adorned with wide venetian blinds and yellow lace curtains. Through these windows I could see the authentic windmill covered with grapevines; the root cellar where potatoes and onions were stored through the winter, and spiders with spooky webs hung overhead; and the general store owned and operated by my family. Also visible were the water tank where Native Americans provided nourishment for thirsty horses, the small store owned by a kind but argumentative bachelor, the cellar for emergency generators, the gasoline pumps, and the unpaved street area where cars and wagon teams parked.

I felt safe within this room, surrounded by love shared by my parents and siblings. Enjoying the solitude, I played with my dolls, read books, and created a fantasy life with paper dolls. The windows provided both comforting sunlight and stargazing opportunities, people to watch, weather to observe, and hours of dreaming about the future.

Interestingly, today I still require light as well as outdoor views for stimulation, security, and centeredness. Whether in a library, a restaurant, or similar indoor setting, I appreciate, whenever possible, not sitting with my back to the door, but positioned so that I can both look out the window and monitor the entryway. Maybe I was meant to be a California sea otter, lying on my back, and comfortably observing the surroundings and spacious blue skies.

Life is filled with another type of window: windows of opportunity for growth, for becoming, for connecting. Whether we ponder life-issues while gazing through windows at peaceful settings, or explore imaginary windows of potential talent and skill, many new dreams and pursuits await our personal cultivation.

Describe a peaceful view observed through a window.

Where can you recapture that peace?

What windows of opportunity await you?

The Vision

I had a vision.
I had a vision in which
I saw my mother.

I had a vision.
I had a vision of my mother speaking to me.

"This year," she said, "your brothers only need two pies,
Cut into eight pieces, then cut again into sixteen pieces.
Thirty-two servings of pie are plenty."

I had a vision.
In my vision, I said,
"Yes, all-wise Mother, I will make two pies, and give
My brothers your instructions about the servings."

I had a vision.
I had a vision that my brothers
Dutifully elected to eat less pie.

I had a vision.
In my vision I saw
My brothers on their knees thanking me
For making only two pies.

I had a vision.
I had a vision that my brothers
Choose to be physically fit
With cholesterol- and fat-free arteries.

I had a vision.
I had a vision that they
Became wiser and wiser
About their health, their well-being.

I had a vision.
I had a vision that my brothers
Made a solemn vow to
Eat more healthfully, walk daily, pray often.

I had a vision.
I had a vision of the future.

Consider significant family members or friends about whom you are concerned.

What avenues, if any, might be taken to assist them?

Well, Hi There!

Six years after her death, I still recall my mother cordially answering the phone by saying, "Well, hi there." How comforting to hear a familiar voice of a person who loved me unconditionally! No matter what the concern or shared news, she was there to listen, to offer encouragement and, on occasion, opinionated advice. Although her words of wisdom were colored with bits and pieces of her own experiences, she lovingly meant well as she shared her thoughts with the hope of making our lives a bit easier and better.

While time eases the loss of a loved one, some memories pain the heart to remember, for familiar experiences no longer exist. Her "Well, hi there!" felt as comfortable as a cub locating its mother, the swallows returning to Capistrano, or a joey cuddled in its mother's pouch. It was the constant in an ever changing world; the poles that steady a tent.

How I miss her voice greeting me with stability and joy! Rarely, could I decipher her physical pain with which she often dealt. When her children called, her time and attention was given to them. However, in her sixties she decided that, unless it was an emergency, she would not telephone her family members. She transferred that responsibility to them. While at the time I thought this to be a harsh choice, I now can appreciate her decision.

Adult children become involved in their own worlds of existence, taking time to call when they have a few minutes of uninterrupted time. Awaiting their calls relieves a parent's frustration of initiating contact only to be faced with voice messages, unanswered emails, or interruptions of their valued family time. After years of child rearing, it may be okay to lay the challenge of connecting and nourishing relationships on the adult children's shoulders. Well, why not? Better to respond with, "Well, hi there!" than unnecessarily disturb their busy lives.

Oh, Mother, how I miss hearing your nurturing voice!

Describe a system of connecting with loved ones.

How does it work for you? What needs to be changed?

When I Was a Teenager

When I was a teenager I saw myself as a delicately protected young adult, raised in part by the holy nuns. Unlike many young children, I lived in a quaint town with only one hundred residents and no secondary school. Again, unlike many young adolescents of high school age, each September I climbed aboard a passenger train to attend an all-girls boarding school in Nebraska, returning home only at Christmas and Easter. I vividly recall rides to and from school on this train, most commonly known as The Galloping Goose. Riding solo in trains, buses, and taxicabs in order to reach a final destination, with amazing trust and nary a fear, may be an almost foreign experience in this twenty-first century. At the very least, I would venture to say that it is so for the majority of adolescents living in the United States.

Cheerleading, softball, basketball, football games? Definitely not! Extracurricular activities consisted of drama plays, musical events, periodic dances, and bus rides into the city for lunch in a Chinese restaurant.

Growing up under the tutelage and guidance of nuns proved to be a time of innocent, insulated protection, like a tropical plant growing in a Colorado greenhouse. Yet the experience also was graced with innumerable personal growth and leadership opportunities. Upon reflection, I view it as a time of unconditional caring, educational challenge, and free-spirited living, with minimal responsibility, except that of taking care of oneself. Additionally, the experience of warm, humid, colorful fall days provided unique memories. Apples never tasted better than those freshly harvested in that part of Nebraska. Wading in the Platte River on senior sneak day seemed, at the time, such a sensible exercise in freedom.

Growing up in a small town created the necessity for unusual, though treasured, experiences. Would I have wished for a more "normal" high school education? *Perhaps*. However, only later in life have I developed a true appreciation of this age-of-innocence opportunity sponsored by my parents and provided by the nuns. It was good. It was meant to be.

Describe an "innocent" growing-up experience that may be a bit foreign to present-day teenagers.

What advise would you share with adolescents growing up in our current society?

Part II

MAKING A DIFFERENCE

(Important Others)

"Make each day useful and cheerful and prove that you know
the worth of time by employing it well. Then youth will be happy,
old age without regret, and life a beautiful success."

Louisa May Alcott (1832-1888)

A Tribute to the O'Reilly Clan

Somewhat like an orange, wherein each individual segment intrinsically is important to the whole, one cannot contemplate a single person in the O'Reilly family without thinking of the entire Irish clan. Therefore, writing about one person without reference to other family members is difficult, if not impossible.

When my beautiful sister, Marie, who is like a second mother to me, fell in love with and married Sean O'Reilly, she presented me with a second father and, subsequently, thirteen "adopted" siblings. Throughout the years, I have felt somewhat like a lost child. Where exactly did I fit? With my biological family where I am the youngest of seven children, but often felt like an "only" with older siblings at boarding school or in the military? Or with my "adopted" family where I chronologically was the oldest, periodically staying with them either to visit or baby-sit the younger children? It felt sort of like being part of a gym class where sometimes you're placed on a certain volleyball team and, on other occasions, assigned to a different group of players.

The beauty and blessing of such an arrangement, however, was that I had numerous memorable experiences in this best-of-both-worlds' position: with older sisters and brothers as they guided and protected me; at other times, with the younger "adopted" siblings who energetically frolicked around playing school, hide and seek, or riding horses. Most vividly, I recall caring for the young children when Marie and Sean speedily traveled fifty miles into town for David's birth; and, on another occasion, to the medical clinic with Molly after she nearly cut off a few fingers in the lawnmower.

Like the orange segments, each child has her or his own special uniqueness. The lyrics to *When Irish Eyes Are Smiling* perceptively describe the beauty of the O'Reilly Clan. Special phrases from the legendary lyrics remind me of my "adopted" siblings: Megan – 'in the lilt of Irish laughter, you can hear the angels sing'; Gretchen – 'with such pow'r in your smile'; James – 'eyes twinkle bright as can be'; Kerry – 'sweet lilting laughter'; Melody – 'your laughter so tender and light'; Molly – 'all the world seems bright and gay'; David – 'smile, like a morn in spring'; Therese – 'Irish hearts are happy'; Katie – 'let us smile each chance we get'; Christopher – 'when Irish eyes are smiling, sure they steal your heart away'; Maggie – 'you should laugh all the while'; Neil – 'your smile is a part of the love in your heart'; Caitlin – 'your smile makes even sunshine more bright'.

Collectively, these human segments formed a family unit tenderly and lovingly cared for by parents who taught them to create fun together through music, storytelling, and game playing. The many singing and guitar engagements of this troupe impressed indelible memories on many audiences. Yet this special blend of voices is witnessed not only in their joy-filled performances, but also in their compassionate, engaging interactions as they support each other through lifetime challenges. Historically, they *are* an exemplary family who pray, play, and work together. Consequently, they remain emotionally and physically connected. Gratefully, I am honored to be an "adopted" member of this exceptional Irish clan.

Tell about a family, other than your own, with whom you have found yourself especially close.

What special characteristics of this family would you like to incorporate into your life?

Aunt Rose

ow do I begin to tell you, Aunt Rose, how much you meant to my family? Your shared love, dedication, and time resulted in your giving lifetime gifts to us: treasured memories of special occasions spent together, support through your infinite wisdom, and areas in which you served as my mentor.

Aunt Rose. You know I don't remember exactly when we began calling you "Aunt Rose." My best guess is that my upbringing taught me that children are to refer to their elders by titles, not just first names. Since you became part of our extended family through marriage, my children and I naturally referred to you as *Aunt* Rose.

We spent memorable holidays and special occasions together. I especially remember the gourmet meal you prepared for us soon after we returned from Germany. It had been three long years since we shared a meal with family, or – as in this case – adopted family members. As a gracious hostess, you opened your arms to us and prepared a beautiful table with food fit for royalty. How can we ever thank you for your willingness to reach out to befriend yet another family, when your own circle of friends and family was so large already? And do you recall all the special birthday celebrations we shared together? I am grateful that we both had January birthdays!

In your roles as mother and career woman, you became a mentor to me. Although I never quite figured out how you managed to "do it all," I tried to emulate your impeccable style of living. Truth be known, before each of your visits, I cleaned house with the energy and determination of a triathlete. Everything you did made a statement about you as a gracious, caring, artistic woman. Family photographs you oil painted are treasured heirlooms.

Since we lived in the same city, there were innumerable times I called you for parenting suggestions. You wisely shared advice that only someone who had successfully raised a family of her own could have given. You modeled Christian parenthood through your commitment, your strong determination to do the best for your family, and, most importantly, your unconditional love. In your kind manner, you assisted others as a mother, mother-in-law, grandmother, friend, and as our special Aunt Rose.

Aunt Rose, how deeply we miss you. But now you have no more pain, can communicate with all your loved ones in heaven as well as on earth, and you are at peace. Truly, I believe that you are with us in spirit. It makes sense that because you helped us on earth, you now guide us in a spiritual way. Please be patient with us as we continue to ask for your wisdom and guidance again – and again – and again.

Tell about a deceased family member or friend to whom you feel especially grateful.

What personal lifelong gifts do you want to share with others?

Brotherhood

Overall, important family and community figures help children with their passage into adulthood by experiencing life together, and through role modeling. Later, significant men and women serve others as mentors to those with families, careers, and relationships on into elderhood. By assisting us with life and death issues, family and friends remain essential to our living the life journey.

My brothers, all four of them, played an integral part in my life drama. While they each exhibit similar gifts of integrity, humor, faith, generosity, and gentlemanly manners, their ornery, a bit mischievous side, seemed more pronounced in childhood years. Collectively, we played baseball, rode horseback or bicycles, milked cows, fed chickens, and played games. Particular incidents, though, come to mind as I recall our growing up years.

In the summertime, the devilishness seemed to grow like bread dough rising in a pan. This yeast quality didn't seem to settle down until the restless spirit gave way to pranks. The hot, dry months presented golden opportunities for putting cornflakes in each other's beds. Frogs mysteriously made their way between bed sheets, just waiting to surprise some weary, unsuspecting soul. Getting into a french-sheeted bed often enough created a suspicious mind-set amongst the seven siblings.

Our normally strict mother tolerated these childhood antics, but Lord have mercy on our souls if we didn't clean up all messes before breakfast! Her guideline, "If you don't clean up your room and make your bed, there will be no afternoon snack!" worked well, as no one wanted to miss a piece of warm homemade bread topped with butter, or a piece of freshly baked pie.

Using "Discipline with Food and Logic" never failed in our household!

Gene holds a special place in my heart because he built me a house in our yard during my early growing-up years. In this dollhouse, I spent hours fussing with my dolls and playing mommy. I *have* wondered if our parents gave him this summer project to keep him busy during his teen years, because today he still teases a lot. Or did he really love his baby sister enough to create this idea from his own free will? It doesn't matter. To me, it served as a wonderful play area during those carefree years.

As a young child, I recall Roy's way with words. He even convinced the family that he should be excused from washing dishes. "Future doctor's hands," he said, "are not to be placed in soapy dishwater!" Likewise, he talked younger siblings into making his bed and doing other chores, paying them with verbal thanks, a smile, nod of the head, or a small pittance. Of course, not doing chores freed him up for more hours of riding horseback, practicing his roping skills, and playing marbles. He also told funny stories at the dinner table, making Charlie laugh so hard that we all got into trouble with you know whom. Roy's tactful bargaining strategies and polished communication skills have served him well in life.

John must be filled with infinite wisdom, for his behavior, I recall, involved quietly listening to conversations and siblings' squabbles. Normally, my father generated dinnertime topics that stimulated creative thinking and discussion. Politics, religion, education, community welfare: all became table topics facilitated by Dad, a self-higher-educated-man. From my vantage point, I viewed John as he ate – and as he listened, absorbing tons of information. He has grown up to become a very wise man. Is there a lesson in his behavior for the rest of us?

And then there's Charlie. Everyone loved Charlie. He laughed at his brothers' stories and shenanigans, and learned to become quite a storyteller himself. The first ten years of our relationship, a rocky time, must have been challenging for our dear mother. While she never allowed arguing in our house, we had plenty of lively discussions in the backyard, by the barn, and chicken coop. Both strong-willed and a wee bit stubborn, we would repeat, "Did not!" "Did too!" like two frogs croaking in a pond. His assignment, a mother-delegated-mission, involved keeping my bicycle in proper working condition. For reasons only known to watchful guardian angels, my tires frequently flattened. One day, frustrated with seemingly constant repairs, he poetically stated, "If you weren't so fat, these tires wouldn't go flat!" Dear Charlie. Everyone still loves him! Even after several decades, I find it comforting to make a telephone call and say, "Hey, Charlie, things are a bit stressful around here. Tell me a funny story to help me lighten up!"

Brothers. They're always there for you!

Share your thoughts about brotherhood.

Describe male figures who had a significant influence on your life.

Caroline: My Student, My Friend

A yellow rose prematurely dying before admirers have absorbed its uniquely created petals, full beauty, and sweet fragrance. A purple lilac blossom lavishly adorning the bush, only to be frozen by an icy spring snowstorm. Such visions remind me of Caroline's transition into eternal life while in her early thirties. Although exhibiting her inner and outer beauty through generous smiles, inquisitive mind, caring manner, and love of life's challenges and rewards, she, like the flowers, was not to realize the mature development of her special gifts.

Through the middle school years, I, as the school counselor assigned to Caroline's academic team, observed her sparkling enthusiasm for life, her energy and excitement for learning, and her lively, sometimes mischievous, manner with her classmates. Her expressive eyes, contagious smile, confidence, and determination constituted admirable qualities that complemented her diverse class of students.

One day, in her mid-twenties, Caroline visited me at school. Such a delightful surprise! As friends, we conversed for more than an hour. Always, I will appreciate that final visit together. She seemed to be pondering many life issues. With an analytical mind, she articulated thoughts about life, as well as the choices and paths taken by several colleagues. Even then, she expressed concern for friends who sought her opinions and guidance. Empathetically, she desired to support them as best she could.

Caroline's journey of the past eighteen months included her family's uncondi-tional devotion and love, her deep faith and trust in the Lord, and her tenacity and stamina through chemotherapy and pain. She accepted God's will for her life and trusted His wisdom and protection for all involved in those final months. Continually thinking of others' needs, her reassuring presence became a gift to many, a model for all to follow.

With Caroline's life an exemplary legacy, she remains forever in the hearts of those blessed by her presence. Now, strengthened with special memories, we, her earthly circle of family and friends, proceed forward in fulfilling God's unknown mission for us.

Review the life of someone who deeply affected your life journey?

What qualities of this person do you seek to emulate?

Fast Reverse

riving east on I-80 with views of soon-to-be-harvested sweet corn and wheat fields, I had five hundred miles of time to contemplate my upcoming high school reunion. Several decades had passed since being with classmates with whom I had experienced learning and good times. Pressing the fast reverse button on an imaginary remote control device enabled me to create a sense of earlier boarding school days in an all-girls school. The innocent and protected, yet loving and caring, environment provided experiences known only to a minute percentage of the population. In this setting, we had opportunities to be intellectually challenged, explore the arts through music and drama, and experience leadership roles through class offices and clubs.

Once the imaginary *play* function began, I remembered dormitory space much like that of a hospital room with only a bed, small dresser, and curtain; inspiring May crowning ceremonies; proms with interesting dates; and walks down a long, steep hill to board a bus into the city. Weekends with non-boarders (known as dayhops) helped ease the loneliness that came with being absent from home for long periods of time.

As I skirted by a small town where people offered refreshments to World War II troops, I recalled a noteworthy boarding school incident. This happened one Sunday afternoon when restless boarders decided to take a leisurely stroll. Within a few blocks of the campus, we noticed a crematorium and cemetery. Daringly, we challenged each other to check out the crematorium. It was tiny, dimly lighted, and contained spooky oven areas. Thinking about it even now sends chills down my spine. Slowly on tiptoe, one after the other, we peeked around and noticed a closed casket. Whispering, we dared each other to open it. Someone nervously, ever so slowly, lifted the lid. Inside was a dead BODY! With eyes widened in shock, we screamed as if in a Halloween haunted house, and scurried out like mice from a starving tomcat. Shakily, we arrived back at the dormitory, promising not to tell the holy Sisters of our mischievous act.

When I arrived at the former boarding school campus, I spent time with those forever friends who still demonstrated fondness for each other by hugging, chatting, laughing, reliving the past, and sharing family updates. We visited the Sisters who had indelibly touched our lives. During the culminating activity for all reunion attendees, we, the milestone honorees, were invited to introduce ourselves and tell about our last fifty years. *Condense the highlights of the past five decades in less than sixty seconds?* I asked myself. It reminded me of completing the exercise, "What do you want on your epitaph?"

Now, a few months after the reunion, I have thought long and hard about that challenging moment. Thus, at the next milestone gathering, I will be prepared for the same invitation to speak about the past. My simple response will be, "I served, I cared, I loved."

Periodically, as I fast reverse to reflect on the past, fast forward to design dreams of the future, then reverse back to the play mode, I realize the importance of concentrating on *play*: enjoying and savoring each precious moment while focusing on relationships with God, family, and friends. In all likelihood, at life's end, our celebration of life – better known as *the funeral* – will focus on a few short clips of our journey. Hmm....Could it be time to give consideration to what I want included in my final life-review?

Describe a reunion or special gathering that stimulated reflection on your own life.

What do you want to remember about the event, the people involved?

Graceful, Faithful Pillars

Penning a writing about Lauren and John for their fiftieth wedding anniversary celebration feels as magnanimous as describing a glorious sunset over the Monterey Peninsula, a breathtaking waterfall in Kauai, or a brilliant rainbow after a torrential Colorado rainstorm. Assuredly, a ream of paper filled by a best-selling author could not give due credit to this graceful, faithful couple who has established themselves as family and community pillars.

With Lauren's artistic grace and John's confident Navy officer stature, this couple has sailed their course based on a deep faith in God as their guide. With our Heavenly Father at the helm, they reared a family, cared for aging parents, helped to build a church, served in civic and church organizations, flipped thousands of buttermilk pancakes, traveled internationally, and explored their own interests and talents. Lauren's oil paintings and John's stained glass pieces are treasured heirlooms of their protective, grateful owners.

More intimate scenarios bring to mind hilarious laughter shared at birthday celebrations, with lighted candle in one lone cupcake; supportive, enlightening conversations involving life and death issues; and tears shed, then inter-mingled, as we hugged and experienced the grieving process after painful losses of loved ones.

Like marble pillars anchoring a structure with graceful beauty while remaining strong and faithful during turbulent storms, this couple moves through life with serene, respectful dignity, and integrity. In pondering their joy-filled and dedicated family unit, one is reminded of Mother Teresa's thoughts on home and family. She states, "If we truly want peace in the world, let us begin by loving one another in our own families. If we want to spread joy, we need for every family to have joy."

Lauren and John are traditional models for couples traveling their life journey together. Their presence is energizing, sending rippling effects of joy and peace to all in their company. Clearly, they are graceful, faithful pillars of the past, present, and future.

Choose a married couple whom you admire and respect.

What marital strategies do you observe that you would like to incorporate into your own relationship?

Harrison: A Hero

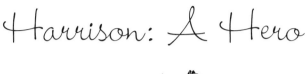

How can one twenty-minute interaction alter a life significantly? Granted, each experience we have changes our life in some way. Yet a recent brief encounter created a moving experience, stimulating my thinking about personal attributes that are most meaningful and forever cherished in this earthly existence.

Visiting Harrison, an almost totally dependent, forty-year old patient with amyotrophic lateral sclerosis (commonly known as Lou Gehrig's disease), I observed qualities of kindness, compassion, patience, and tenacity. Laboriously speaking to me or spelling out words, he shared bits and pieces of his life. With sparkling, dark brown eyes, he spoke about his two daughters, and invited me to view a colorful calendar portraying their pictures. Determined to stimulate his brilliant mind, Harrison continues to learn by listening to audiobooks, using the computer, and interacting with others through the written or spoken word. His competitive spirit, honed in races as a cyclist, may be energizing him for struggling through each day of existence.

This life-enriching visit reminded me that regardless of our physical, environmental, or emotional situation, we *can* find meaning in our life, control our attitude, stimulate learning, and proceed through our journey with kindness and compassion. Additionally, it brought to mind one of my favorite books, *Man's Search for Meaning,* by Dr. Viktor E. Frankl, wherein the author-psychiatrist describes his three-year experience as a prisoner at Auschwitz and other Nazi concentration camps. Learning that human beings *can* find meaning and a sense of responsibility in life, regardless of circumstances, pain, or suffering, helped the author survive a gruesome period in his life.

Through his presence, Harrison exemplifies respect, caring, and perseverance in living, while modeling empathy for others. Such qualities will live on forever in the memory of people touched by his life. I am grateful to the hero Harrison, for through his very existence, his spirit, his being, he demonstrates the attributes of a successful man.

Ultimately, Harrison taught me that it is not what we do nor what we accomplish, but *who we are* – the hospitable manner in which we interact with others, our compassionate service to the human race, the continued stimulation of our mind and spirit – that makes a difference in this diverse world.

Describe someone who has a debilitating disease.

What have you learned from observing this person's daily struggles?

If I Saw You Again

If I saw you again, I would say, "Tell me about your life. Has it been good to you? Have you been happy? Have you no regrets that it didn't work out for us; that it was the wrong time in your life, and in my college career?"

If I saw you again, we'd meet in a quiet cafe with a cozy garden patio overlooking a gentle stream. Relaxed, with time not an issue, we would share memories of our separate lives since we parted decades ago: the experiences of sorrow, excitement, and joy since those early days, those late teen years.

If I saw you again, I would ask, "Why? Why couldn't you wait two more years until I earned my college degree? Why did you choose not to wait, but instead find another woman with whom to share your life?"

But wait a moment. Now it is all coming back to me. During that period, you had experienced many losses in a brief span of time: the sudden death of your mother, the farm machinery accident, my attending college over four hundred miles away.

If I saw you again, I would tell you how desperately ill I became after reading your "Dear John" letter. I was so overcome with grief; I could not get out of bed for three days. Regretfully, I returned your class ring, mailing it with both sadness and love.

Yet if I saw you again, I would acknowledge my gratitude for our treasured, innocent, and carefree times together. Giving a friendly hug, I then would depart, sharing sincere wishes for peace and contentment on the last segment of your life journey.

Perhaps before leaving this earthly world, we *shall* meet again. Time alone will unfold the unknown future events. In the meantime, my very dear friend, may God travel with you.

By mentally turning back the hands of time, select a person about whom you cared deeply.

Consider an imaginary rendezvous with that person: Where would you meet? What would you say?

If I Were an Artist

How can this be? Is this real? Has Cecilia really left us for eternal life with God? Wasn't it just yesterday that our birthday group enjoyed dinner together, laughing from the depths of our souls over humorous cards? When, true to tradition, she and Paul each filled a cone with ice cream so tall and fully packed? Did she even notice that Gene, John, Lauren, and I walked out of the restaurant first, too embarrassed to look at them licking cones like little kids in an amusement park?

Cecilia certainly knew the secret of making the most of each day! How did she confidently manage to be open to every new experience of life's journey? I believe it was Picasso that said we spend the first fifty years of our life learning how to be an adult, and the last fifty years learning how to be a child. Somehow, though, I think she allowed the child within her to be a daily part of her life journey.

If I were Picasso, or any artist, attempting to design an appropriate setting for Cecilia's portrait, I would paint snowcapped mountains that she had either climbed or skied – and in which she had camped, hunted, and fished. Somewhere in the landscape would be an airplane, a car, train, cruise ship, and hot air balloon, depicting her love for global travel.

Cecilia would be standing in the middle of a garden masterfully planted with a variety of vegetables and flowers, some of which were sweet corn, artichokes, and roses. I would paint her in a canary yellow beekeeper's suit, and wearing tap-dance shoes, to make for a quick change of activities! She would have pliers in an upper pocket just in case she had a few extra moments for making a rosary or two, and a big white handkerchief in the back pocket for wiping teary eyes and runny noses. Cecilia would be playing a base fiddle, with a violin and piano nearby waiting their turn. Twelve energetic children would be stationed in various parts of the garden, working their rows while listening to the music of this multi-talented lady who tried to do it all.

If I were an artist, I would paint Cecilia's inner spirit of love, empathy, and peace. Somehow I would try to capture her welcoming, loving smile, and the look of contentment that only comes from a peaceful heart; the caring eyes of a concerned caregiver; the hands browned from the sun and aged from years of labor as she raised a large family.

If I were an artist, I would title my painting, "Our Teacher, Our Friend" for, in living, she taught us to listen; to be available for other's needs; to pray, laugh, hug, and smile. In the process of dying, she taught us to be open to yet another adventure in life's journey; to lean on one another; to feel the pain of loss together.

If I were an artist, I would never part with Cecilia's portrait, but place it strategically where each day viewers could be reminded that we need to live each day as if it were our last; and that we – like her – will be born into life eternal.

Write about a close relative or friend who is no longer on earth.

Explore personal characteristics of this person that drew you close to her or him.

Reflections on Love

Love is humble, truthful, respectful.

Love is having both separate and common goals.

Love is giving, sharing, caring, forgiving.

Love is being interested and engaged in another's life.

Love is both leading and following.

Love is understanding that relationship is a process.

Love is flexible and open-minded to new, varied ideas.

Love is allowing space to develop as an individual,
the person God intended one to be.

Love is exploring new adventures and interests.

Love is taking time to enjoy special moments together.

Love is accepting change in one another.

Love is maintaining a sense of humor,
especially through challenging experiences.

Love is taking care of oneself – fostering a mental, spiritual,
and physical well-being.

Love is placing God at the center of our lives,
believing and trusting in His guidance and unconditional love.

Create your own "Reflections on Love."

*In defining your own beliefs above "love," what did you
learn about yourself?*

ternally, I will be grateful for the precious minutes Ruth and I spent together a few days before she left this world to be with God, her beloved husband, relatives, and friends. During those final moments, I was able to thank her for being my caregiving mentor. We talked about her caring for her father, multiple family members, and many friends from the church and neighborhood. For these people, she would cook meals, drive them to various appointments, counsel, console, and encourage them. I shared my gratitude for her modeling the traits of a gracious hostess, for a person always felt welcome as she opened the door and cheerily said, "Come on in!" She replied, "I always liked to visit with folks." Truth is, she loved people and used her many talents in caring for them.

Through her example, Ruth taught me to pray. Many times during the day she whispered the prayer, "Lord, you have got to help me. I can't do this alone." She shared that the Lord was even with her as she placed each ice cube tray filled with water into the freezer – a nearly impossible task for a ninety-three-year-old person with limited eyesight. Proudly, she pointed her finger and, with that convincing look on her face and determined voice, said, "You know, I never spilled a drop. *He* was there helping me!" She prayed for His guidance as she – with much effort at times – cooked meals, felt her way through the house, and struggled to care for herself.

Having lived through the Depression and several war years, Ruth was part of a great generation of women, women who labored and saved money to pay expenses. Diligently, impeccably, and respectfully caring for Mother Earth, she designed a beautiful landscape of flowers, grapevines, shrubs, and trees, leaving lasting beauty for others to enjoy. Like pioneer women of her era, she had a deep faith in God; firm convictions about living a moral, Christian life of integrity; and a strong character that enabled her to deal tenaciously with many issues on her journey.

What is a person to do, now that one's mentor of spirituality, courage, and generosity is no longer physically present? Where do we turn for guidance, for sharing of concerns, for insight into living life? We can keep fresh our memories of Ruth living a prayerful life, a life of doing for others while she cared for herself with wisdom and fortitude. In modeling her legacy, we can create our own joyful memories with each person we meet on our path to eternity.

Reflect on someone you admire. Write or discuss her or his exemplary qualities.

What are special qualities or abilities you would like to foster within yourself?

Sisterhood

When on trips to various locations, I like to browse through publications in lobbies, hotel rooms, and cottages. Most recently, while journeying to Nova Scotia, I read an article on female generations which stated that *character* and *ambition* were two characteristics handed down through women. The concept kept pestering me, like a kitten waiting to be cuddled and stroked. Thoughts about my own heritage kept fading in and out, as does the sun on a partially cloudy day.

After meeting Susan, owner of the Rose Blossom Cottages, it became real to me that women with strong character and ambition, once they find their niche, can be most successful. Susan's special talents, integrity, and ambition characterize her uniqueness as a businesswoman. With vision and entrepreneurial spirit, this creative woman remodeled several cottages on peaceful St. Mary's Bay. Using artistic flair and design as well as hours of labor, she transformed run-down buildings into homey cottages with interior and exterior ambience, offering guests both comfort and pleasure.

Okay, then, what unique qualities have been handed down in my family? While I never met my paternal female ancestors, my father shared stories that helped shape my mental pictures of them. My great-grandmother remained in Ireland while her husband came to the United States for employment. After a year or so, he sent enough ocean passage funds for her and several children. Leaving family and homeland, they made the long, tedious voyage only to be greeted with the news that he had died. Widowed and living in an Irish ghetto, she struggled to care for her family. After a few years she remarried. To withstand these physical and emotional hardships, she must have been a tenacious, determined, hard-working woman.

My paternal grandmother, an artistically and musically talented woman, was described as spiritually devout, soft-spoken, and a community caregiver. Her charcoal pencil drawing completed in the late 1800's depicts much personal insight and spiritual depth. As a piano teacher, she gave lessons to her son and daughter. My dad said, "I didn't like to practice, especially when my friends were outside playing baseball, but," he continued, "I'll always be grateful to my mother for insisting that I practice my music before playing games." He made a lifelong habit of playing the piano, giving pleasure to many listeners.

My maternal great-grandmother, an immigrant from Czechoslovakia, homesteaded on the Kansas prairie. Hearing legendary stories of her enduring harsh weather and rearing eleven children, I would envision her to be physically strong, with exceptional strength in character. One of her daughters, my grandmother, continued life on the South Dakota prairie. She was a gentle, creative, and kind homemaker. With oven temperature tested by placing her hand inside a wood stove, she baked buttermilk biscuits and chokecherry pie, her signature dishes. An ambitious craftsperson, she made many quilts, knitted, and crocheted items for family, friends, and non-profit organizations. Once, while I was on a weekend visit with her in her small log home, a major storm developed, resulting in my being snowed in with her for two weeks. It became a special time for learning to sew, cook, play games, and sleep in her big bed, as well as tramp through the snow to the outhouse (or use the chamber pot!).

My beloved mother, a woman of notable internal strength and dedication to her family and community, was especially supportive of women. In the spirit of volunteerism, she organized sewing circles for women who gathered regularly for sewing, doing handiwork, and making quilts. At times, the finished products would be used as prizes for raffles, bingo, and card parties. These sewing circles later became County Home Extension Clubs. After her seven children were grown, she volunteered for seventeen years, teaching 4-H members to sew, do leatherwork, knit, and crochet.

Perhaps Mother's internal strength began to take shape in her early child-hood, when she was taught to "be strong and not show sorrow"; at age six, to live with a family in a small town fifty miles away in order to attend school. I find it difficult to fathom what it would have been like to experience leaving home at that young age, returning only for Christmas and summer holidays. Yes, her independent spirit, strong will, and commitment to serving others evolved from early childhood experiences and the familial values and beliefs instilled by her parents.

In reality, my sisters, over a decade older than I, were like second mothers until I was in my early forties. This stage in life, when individuals more readily accept themselves as unique instead of emulating others or living in their shadows, becomes a welcome, freeing period. Although we had a few trips together as sisters, only recently, now that our children are grown, have we taken more freedom to do sister-things. As an "if I had my life to do over item," I would have encouraged annual outings, without children and husbands, to foster needed female support and the enjoyment of sisterhood.

Sisterhood. Its spirit is felt worldwide: through a smile, an encouraging word, time together, or a fund raising event like the Run for a Cure. It is real. It is out there, promoting support, peace, kindness, and compassion amongst all inhabitants of Mother Earth.

In which ways has sisterhood affected your life?

How can you be a promoter of sisterhood?

Tuesdays with Natalie

For the past nine months, Tuesdays became special days; hours devoted to spending time with Natalie, her children Katie and Patrick, and Grandma Lauren. Together we laughed, played, listened to music, took trips to the park, ate lunch, shared stories, changed diapers, put kids down for naps, washed clothes, changed beds, and straightened cupboards. Even Katie helped to make the beds, as well as place folded bibs and dishtowels in their designated drawers. Patrick continued to entertain and amaze us with his learning to walk, talk, and make up his own mind about which foods to eat, invariably pushing away any morsel that looked like a vegetable. With favorite music playing, the children danced and waved hands in motion to the rhythms and meanings of the lyrics. Natalie, in her soft-spoken, kind-but-firm manner, guided the children as they played, looked at books, put together puzzles, learned to count and recognize alphabet letters, and ate their meals. Her expressive eyes danced with pride and love as she watched her children and told stories about them.

The women, of course, had snatches of time during the busy day in which to share stories of growing up, families, children, religion, and recipes. Sometimes we even pondered our husbands: What makes them the way they are? From which planet did they come? One day we conversed about Natalie's admirable athletic ability. She explained, "In growing up, the ten children frequently played games, danced, had lots of parties, and basically made their own fun." Then she added, "In high school, we could only choose one sport, so I selected basketball because it lasted the longest!" She and her brother Terrence seemed to have an especially close relationship. When I asked how this happened to be, she replied, "It all began with communicating as we milked cows together. We talked about a lot of things then."

Never have I witnessed someone so patiently resigned and open to God's divine plan. Natalie's deep faith, love of God, and daily commitment to prayer and bible study gave her great strength to endure the unknown future. While the outcome of her diagnosis and treatment was uncertain, she – with the help of Joseph, their families, church community, friends, and neighbors – lived through each day with earnest hope and faithful love. Physically and emotionally caring for one another, they all supported their common mission together. Similar to a host of pioneers bracing a fence being threatened by an eighty-mile-an-hour wind, or a crew of sailors struggling to steady a vessel as it rocks back and forth between frightfully forceful waves, they remained strong.

Tuesdays with Natalie were filled with love; with working together to care for the family; with laughter and smiles that helped to lighten the emotional and physically-challenged loads; and with praying together in thanksgiving for God's many blessings. My Tuesdays with Natalie will never be forgotten, especially the shared hugs and sincere "I love you's."

No longer suffering, Natalie's precious spirit rests in peace with God. Stationed at the earth-to-eternity crossing, poised to greet us when it is our transition time, she patiently awaits a reunion with those dearest to her heart.

Describe an important other in your life.

How has this person enhanced your life journey?

Yum Yum Time

Today resulted in a real memory test, a live trivial pursuit game, if you will. Recalling experiences from fifty years ago became "Do you remember when…? What ever happened to…? Did I really look like that?" conversation topics.

My former classmates and I laughed as we recalled the nuances of the good Sister who monitored our behavior. On occasion, she allowed us to view TV programs – the black and white version, of course – approved by her. She often encouraged us to watch her favorite Loretta Young Show. One time, however, the admired star wore an off-the-shoulder gown. Sister quickly jumped out of her chair, stood in front of the screen, holding the folds of her long skirt out to each side so that we could not see the "immodest" actress. Soon thereafter, she wrote a letter to Miss Young praising her program's quality, but suggesting that she dress more appropriately for her viewers. Then, she proceeded to strongly urge us all to sign the letter – which, naturally, we did. In those early formative years, we were such innocent souls. How significantly mores have changed in fifty years!

The dear Sister, now in her nineties, still talks about the fine Loretta Young Show and I Love Lucy programs. My best guess is that she does not watch many current TV shows, as she devotes most of her time to art projects, reading books, and responding to her hotmail.com messages.

With renewed friendship after a lengthy void, my classmates and I vowed to remain connected and supportive in whatever issues may develop in the next fifty years. Well, maybe thirty years is a bit more realistic target.

After the poignant, lengthy luncheon with three high school classmates, two of whom I had not seen in five decades, I took a meditative walk and then treated myself to a sinful piece of snicker cheesecake. Halfway through the heavenly dessert, a woman walked by and said, "Isn't that delicious?"

"Yes," I responded, "but I'm feeling guilty eating each bite."

"You only live once," she responded.

"I know," I nodded.

The reality of this statement rang true today, in particular, as I lunched with my dear friends. After reviewing the lives of former classmates already deceased; of ill, then dying spouses; and of children who are no longer with us, I felt the need to reenergize the body with something deliciously sweet. Sitting on the restaurant patio in the warmth of the late afternoon sun refreshed the spirit. The fresh air, sinful dessert, and time alone to process the special luncheon gathering replenished my body, mind, and spirit with energy, and served as a reminder to relish each moment of life.

Yum, yum. Cheesecake never tasted so good!

Recall a get-together with classmates.

What special facets of the occasion do you want to remember?

Part III

BECOMING MORE AWARE

(Personal Growth)

"Small things, done in great love, bring joy and peace."

Mother Teresa of Calcutta (1910-1997)

A Tip of the Hat

Once in a while on my daily walks, though not often, a man tips his hat as he passes me. Each time, it brings back memories of my father. For always, whether walking in our small village, or visiting another location in the world, he tipped his hat as he passed a woman. My best guess is that he received training in this manner of greeting as a young child.

My mother, on the other hand, had a strong belief about the wearing of hats. Her rule was short and to the point: "Hats are not to be worn in the house!" Only one time do I ever recall her making an exception to this hard and fast rule. During a Thanksgiving holiday, thirteen adult family members returned home to celebrate this feast. However, sometimes plans change mid-stream. When someone discovered the sewer backing up in the basement, the focus suddenly switched from relaxed family togetherness to the water supply and bathroom facilities.

With living in the country and this being a holiday time, a plumber could not make the fifty-mile trip to my parents' home until two days later. When he finally did arrive, we learned that the roots of lilac bushes blocked proper flow through the pipes.

The two-day interim, when guests could not take showers, was of great concern to the visiting granddaughter's fiancé. Embarrassed by his somewhat oily and unruly hair, Bill donned a baseball cap before coming to the breakfast table. The rest of us were well aware of Mom's rule and nervously awaited her sergeant major reaction. When Mom came out of the kitchen to the dining room and saw this 6' 2" young man sitting at the table with protective cap on his head, she commanded, "Hats are not to be worn inside the house!"

"But, my hair…," Bill stuttered to his soon-to-be grandmother-in-law.

"Oh, all right," she stated begrudgingly. "Because the sewer is acting up, I guess you may be excused this time." The rest of the family, with heads bowed and eyes still staring at their plates, smiled in amazement that Mom made this exception to her firm rule. *Hmmm,* I thought. *Maybe it is true that people soften with age.*

Manners, it seems, are best learned in early childhood. Responding punctually to invitations, calling before stopping by someone's house, respecting others' space when using cell phones, promptly sending thank-you notes – or at the very least extending a verbal expression of gratitude – are just a few examples of proper etiquette. Presently, it seems, some social graces are not practiced as fastidiously as in my growing up years. Though sometimes ignored, I believe people's manners still remain important to a society. When exercised, hospitable practices make for a kinder, more compassionate world. Isn't it, then, worth our effort to use them as a daily practice wherever we are, whatever we are doing?

Describe specific manners learned as a child.

What current daily practices need to be honed in an effort to respect other people?

A View from the Bleachers

As if sitting in the bleachers observing a dynamic softball game, I watched the eyes of a terminally ill mother as she focused on one child, then the other. Proudly, she observed each scenario of the children as they played on the teeter-totter, slithered down the slide, danced to music, and even engaged in slightly warm sibling discussions over toys and books. Patiently, in a soft-spoken manner, she guided them as they learned to walk, talk, feed themselves, play with educational toys, and pray.

With calm determination, Kim explained to Lisa the potty training do's and don'ts, rewarding success with encouraging praise. Several caregivers assisted the three-year-old with this school-of-hard-knocks' experience. Although dealing with a terminal illness and walking with a cane, the mother remained consistent with her message, sometimes employing time-out consequences. As a mother and educator, she realized the importance of teaching choices, decisions, consequences, and responsibility.

Andy, on the other hand, mimicked words and gestures in his young toddler way. A cuddler, he loved to lay his head on his mother's breast as she swayed back and forth while sitting in a chair, carefully protecting him with her right, unparalyzed arm. With family and friends providing the majority of his care since birth, I cannot comprehend the happiness Kim felt in those limited priceless moments.

As a grandstand observer, I witnessed pure joy, determination, patience, love, and overwhelming kindness within this home-stadium. I heard biblical children's songs played on the stereo as mother watched and sang with the little ones. I believe Kim's heart was filled with hope and confidence that Lisa and Andy would live their lives as she did, with a deep faith in God and trust in the ever-present Lord.

Describe a personal observation of an ill person that made an indelible mark on your mind.

What did you learn from this experience?

Alone in the Lake

The park was unusually quiet that day. The mile-long walking path which surrounds the lake was iced over from the recent cold weather, yet enjoyed by the geese as they strutted gingerly over its smooth surface. Typically, other walkers and joggers share the walking path as they exercise, watch birds, and absorb the beauty of the snowcapped mountains. Not today, for it noticeably was serene with only two of us on the path.

About seventy feet past the old dock area of the lake, I noticed an abundance of geese on the ice. Then, I heard, "Help! Help!" Scanning the area in an effort to locate the voice, I saw a small head bobbing up and down about fifty feet from the shore.

"Oh God!" I thought. *"Somebody's fallen through the ice! Someone is alone in the lake!"*

"We can't go on the ice," shouted my friend who was following not far behind. "It's too thin!"

Heart pounding and frightened that someone might be close to giving up, I screamed, "We're going to get help! Hang in there! Keep your head above the ice! It's going to be okay!" Anxious for immediate help, I looked to the nearby parking area behind me, noticing one lone van. I prayed, *Please, Lord, let someone be in the vehicle!*

I ran to the van, knocked on the window and desperately shouted, "Help! Is anyone in there?" A man raised himself from a reclined position. He appeared to be relaxed as he listened to the radio. Again I screamed, "Help! Someone's fallen through the ice! Do you have a cell phone?"

"Yes," he responded.

"Thank God," I exclaimed. "Hurry! Call for help! Someone has fallen through the ice. Someone is alone in the lake."

As he placed the call to 911, I ran back to the shore, again screaming at the top of my lungs, "You're going to be okay! Help is on the way! Try to hang on to the ice!" I kept repeating encouraging messages, attempting to make contact with the person whom I feared was losing both strength and courage. Each time the person's head went under water, I prayed that she or he would have the energy and willpower to rise above the ice and keep from drowning.

I thought to myself, *Oh, hurry! Hurry! This person is not going to make it much longer!* I desperately prayed that resources would arrive in time to save this precious life.

After what seemed like an eternity, but in reality was only a few minutes, the emergency vehicle arrived. An ambulance followed shortly thereafter. When one of the rescue party members started walking on the ice, it cracked and he fell into the water a few feet from the shore. Quickly, other rescuers tied a rope around him, and he once again proceeded cautiously, pushing a sled along the side. Reaching the person, he successfully placed him on the sled and, with the assistance of the other emergency workers, pulled him to shore. How bitterly cold and frightfully scared looked this lad of about eight years of age. *My God*, I thought. *He could have been one of our grandchildren!*

The ambulance personnel proceeded to wrap him in blankets and place him in their vehicle. With the young lad safely in the rescue workers' care, I shook hands with the man from the van who placed the initial emergency call from his cell phone, and said, "Thanks for your help!"

My friend and I continued our walk, reliving the life-threatening experience in the quiet solitude of our thoughts.

Prior to this harrowing ordeal, I sometimes wondered how I would react in an emergency situation such as we had just witnessed. Now I realize that one responds instinctively within seconds, attempting everything in one's power to gain quick assistance.

Sometimes, I wonder about the boy that nearly drowned on that frigid January afternoon. *Where does he live? Does he have brothers and sisters? What does he remember about his near-death experience?*

Have you assisted with saving a victim from tragedy?

What did you learn about yourself from the experience?

Easter Gifts

$\mathcal{M}$onths ago, who would have predicted that one might be fitness walking in an Easter snowstorm? Yet that is exactly what happened in an attempt to exercise on Easter Saturday. During the previous night, the spring snowstorm gifted us with fourteen inches of snow. But today, this storm-ending still offers snowflakes which Coloradoans, after two years of severe drought, regard as white gold. As I walked, I noticed that, ever so gently, the ponderosa pine, Douglas fir, and Colorado spruce boughs lifted their snow-laden gifts to the heavens.

Experiencing eye contact with one of God's creatures, the coyote, became another priceless gift. As I walked toward the livery at the YMCA Camp, I stealthily and slowly observed this furry animal gracefully crossing the road about twenty yards ahead. Several times it slowed its pace to watch my movements, then stopped near a moss-covered boulder, and lay down in the snow. Cautiously observing me from this position, it awaited my next move. We both seemed fixated on the moment: the coyote analyzing this first-time guest of its protected terrain; and I, in awe, admiring the beauty and uniqueness of this creature. I wondered, *How could anyone harm such a graceful animal?*

Pausing in the quiet of the surroundings, I was reminded of a 22-caliber rifle hanging above the kitchen door of our family home. Dad, in his wisdom, kept it high out of his children's reach, firmly instructing us not to touch the gun. I recall quizzically looking at it from time to time, respecting its power from a distance. You see, it was because of the coyotes that my father decided to place a loaded gun in a strategic location, a point that was closest to the back door.

This area allowed quick access to shoot these creatures that sometimes robbed our chicken coop, depriving us of both eggs and needed meat. Chickens were raised to provide food for our large family, not for the coyotes. In his integrity, Dad only chose to shoot the coyotes when they came to invade the necessary food supply for his wife and seven children.

As I stood in silence those few snowy minutes, I gave thanks for sharing the unforgettable moments, though different, with the coyote. Experiencing the solitude of the area, the moist snowflakes on the face, and the exchanged glances between person and creature became priceless Easter gifts.

Describe a moment in time for which you are grateful.

What childhood memory did the event elicit?

Going with the Flow

W)here...when...how can I stimulate, direct, and shape the stream of artistic energy coming from within? While an abundance of ideas are "out there" or "in there," each artist must create her or his own system for generating and maneuvering the flow, like strategically steering a canoe through streams, rapids, or calm waters.

The *place* for creative energy flow is critical. I find my best writing takes place near water, whether it is a city pond, reservoir, mountain stream, or near the ocean. In these locations, the sound of water flowing and waterfowl quacking and honking provide stimulation for spontaneous release of inner thoughts.

Timing is critical also. As I sit, dressed in a housecoat and sipping strong hot coffee, my creative juices begin to flow best in the day's early hours, before other home inhabitants arise. Mainly, this time is used for spiritual journaling, brainstorming creative topics, outlining ideas, or reading. Additionally, it is a positive time for constructive proofing, wordsmithing, and editing volumes of drafts. Later in the afternoon or evening seems to be an optimal time for inputting handwritten originals and reworking drafts on the computer, getting them ready for critiquing the next morning, or during the day at a park, library, or quiet cafe.

Both *place and time*, therefore, become important for expanding creative topics. Whether near water, the mountains, or city parks, the creative spirit flows forth in an abundance of thoughts from deep within the soul.

In addition to important time and place criteria, the *mind, body* and *spirit* need to be in balance for ultimate creativity. Physical exercise, prayer, spiritual journaling, philanthropic efforts, a peaceful countenance all set the stage for the creative stream to flow in a positive direction. Setting realistic goals and timelines furnishes the required framework for writing projects. Finally, connecting with supportive and encouraging fellow-artists, as well as reading materials about creative interests, assists in igniting the enthusiasm and energy necessary for projects.

Defining one's strategies for creativity and incorporating them into the day's schedule promote a "going with the flow" technique needed for productivity. With necessary place, timing, and physical as well as spiritual balance, I am able to proceed forward with persistence, energy, and structure, allowing the muse to navigate the flow of ideas to a project's completion.

Describe the optimal place, time, and balance for your creative work.

What new strategies might enhance your creative talent and productivity?

Grandchildren as Professors

Reflecting upon what I learned from my grandchildren resulted in a few surprises, the most revealing of which is that they taught me everything I need to live in this world. Really – truly – it's a fact! How can this be? Perhaps innocently observing people and nature, coupled with experiencing varied events and emotions, they quickly learn survival skills for their life journey. These basic, common-sense guidelines gathered early in life, like precious gems of wisdom, might serve all people well.

Once, while my four-year-old grandson Danny visited us, he happened to pass by the bathroom as I brushed my teeth. The faucet remained turned on. With great concern and excitement in his voice, he exclaimed, "Grandma, don't waste the water!" Oh, oh – wake-up call. At this early age, he recognized the need for humans to care for Mother Earth. After all, they are only using her for a few short years.

A special treat last summer was a visit from granddaughter Annette. Relishing in having some alone time away from siblings and parents, she spent quiet moments playing with toys, reading books, and doing art projects. Unaware of her perceptive observations, I continued with my household responsibilities. One day, as I prepared the evening meal, she softy said, "Grandma, you don't smile very much, do you?" Another wake-up call. Her remark caught me by surprise, as my inner self obviously had become translucent in the eyes of this young child. Since hearing her feedback, I have tried to be more cognizant of the power of smiling. Although a person may be dealing with physical, emotional, or mental trauma, wearing a smile somehow, almost like a bit of instant magic, lightens the pain.

When young grandson Scott attempted a new experience of trying out for the school musical, he surprised his family with his determination, his soon-to-be-discovered natural talent, and unpretentious sharing of his gift. While witnessing his performance, I became reminded of the importance of nurturing our creative selves, taking risks in order to grow, and generously sharing our time and talents with other people.

Being both assertive and accepting of others, my granddaughter Juliana confidently thinks through her values and beliefs and stays firm in her commitments. Learning to weigh multiple viewpoints and stand tall in her choices, she uses the skills of listening, timing, and acceptance of other peoples' opinions and personalities. Above all, she teaches me the value of prayer in one's life, especially the importance of praying for patience with our ever-changing selves and that of others.

My granddaughter Molly is especially observant of the world about her and of people's feelings and actions. Even at age five, she taught me the importance of recognizing physical as well as emotional boundaries. Becoming aware of surroundings and labeling landmarks, a strategy for living sensibly and defensively, seemed to be a natural instinct for her. Molly also intuitively knows that being cognizant of the needs of others and honoring their space makes for a respectful cohabitation of our world.

To enjoy life to its fullest captures the essence of Claire, a grandchild from the midwest. Almost from birth, she eagerly pursued new adventures through crafts, music, athletics, and raising animals as well as vegetables. That zest for undertaking learning, experimenting, and practicing a skill seems inherent in her being. She teaches me to enjoy the journey while honing and sharing talents with others.

"I'll do it myself!" became the mantra initiated at age three by all the grandchildren. My granddaughter Gretchen, though, particularly exhibited determination to be independent before the average onset of do-it-yourselfers. She knew what she wanted (set goals) and eagerly, sometimes stubbornly, set about getting her needs met (accomplish the task). Pouring milk in a bowl of cereal, fixing a peanut-butter sandwich, and dressing herself became her daily routine earlier than most children.

Such independence reminds me of all my grandchildren who learned home-making chores beginning at age three. They prepared their school lunches by age five, washed and dried their own clothes by age ten, and learned to care for their belongings early-on. Mastered in childhood, these life-long skills of caring for a home, nourishing our bodies, and being responsible for our choices travel with us into adulthood, our careers, and retirement. Able adults, like able children, who allow others to unnecessarily care for them steal from their reservoirs of self-confidence, self-esteem, and independence.

I am grateful for lessons taught by my precious grandchildren: caring for Mother Earth; using the power of a smile; sharing our God-given time and talents; establishing boundaries and living respectfully; exploring new interests and enjoying the journey; living purposefully, independently, and responsibly; and living assertively while praying for patience in accepting others' choices. If all human beings were to implement these basic criteria for living life, perhaps we might live more contentedly and peacefully with one another.

Most grandchildren have a unique acceptance of their grandparents as human beings. They view them as fun-loving caregivers, whom they sometimes place on imaginary pedestals. In like manner, grandparents foster a special relationship with their children's offspring. Because of all the lessons they have taught me, I, without hesitation, proudly promote my grandchildren to the honorary status of Professors in Living Life.

Define successful-living strategies learned from children.

What lessons might you incorporate into your own life?

esearching a subject, preparing a presentation, and delivering it to an audience remains a vital interest of mine. The challenge, effort, and results seem similar to an athlete who focuses intently with enthusiasm and persistence to succeed.

Early in my career as a school counselor, I presented the topic of Success at a conference. It seemed a natural fit after years of teaching Organization, Motivation, and Goal-Setting Strategies to middle school students and parents. With a burning drive to offer a stimulating session, I read literature, listened to audio cassettes, and surveyed a group of adults about the meaning of success and what it takes to succeed. After completing handouts and presentation materials, I felt quite prepared.

The well-received program began with the theme music from "Top Gun" and ended with Whitney Houston's "Greatest Gift of All." According to evaluations, highlights of the program included the multi-media materials, interactive and engaging exercises, and the quality of subject information and handouts.

Most presenters, however, are wise enough to realize that, in any given audience, a few people will nod off to sleep, chat with their neighbors, or make out the grocery list, as has been known to occur during middle school faculty meetings. In contrast, those interested and engaged in my presentation maintained good eye contact with the speaker, followed along with the exercises, and conscientiously took notes. It pleased me that participants made notations throughout the presentation, for a person taking notes is always a positive indication that information is being well received. It results in one of those two thumbs up,

"Yes!" moments.

Today, some years past that conference session, I am concerned about the eager learners who recorded the meaningful definitions of success as defined by famous personalities. You see, now I am wiser, and realize that an individual's success depends on one's own personal definition, not that authored by another. While other people's thoughts may be used as guides, they are not the ultimate criteria for personal success. It all has to do with setting unique goals and timelines. Only the individual truly knows when she or he has attained success. Naturally, when a group establishes a goal by consensus, then the success-criteria is determined collectively.

Successful people come in different shapes and sizes. Perhaps it is a baby who learns to crawl; a non-English speaking laborer earning enough to pay the bills each week; a homeless person who finds food and shelter for the evening; a patient with Lou Gehrig's disease just making it through another day; a cancer patient surviving one more moment. "Success" then becomes like "old," – a relative, challenging-to-define term. It's such a personal thing.

Perhaps as an overall strategy for success, one might establish various goals: an overall lifetime goal, and secondary five-year and one-year goals. Attaining these specific benchmarks might, then, be termed "Success." For example: "I will be successful when I walk twenty miles each week." The achieved goal translates into success, as defined by the creator of the goal. Likewise, those "I did it!" and pat-on-the-back moments become rewards for personal successes.

Sure wish I could do that presentation over again. Oh, well, the participants have probably discovered the true meaning of success by now. They, too, are becoming wiser with each passing year.

Consider a definition for success that has personal meaning for you.

In which areas have you felt successful?

In the Beginning, In the End

Joy, tearful pain, pride, hurt, relieved, worry, inspired, grateful. Is it possible to feel these eight emotions during a single episode? For some individuals, yes, especially when the occasion involves attending a memorial service for the parent of toddlers.

If a person had a special relationship with the deceased, she or he harbors *joy* that their paths have crossed along the way. Nonetheless *tearful pain* erupts like a volcano knowing that hugs and earthly communication are but a memory of the past; the exchanged "I love you's" no longer audible.

One cannot help but feel *pride* for this admirable woman who fought the cancer battle with tenacity similar to that of a Tour de France cyclist. It *hurts* to realize that the efforts of chemotherapy and radiation failed to shrink the inoperable tumor, saving the life of a mother who desperately longed to care for her children.

Notably observable on the faces of relatives and friends are silent expressions of *worry* regarding the unknown future. The minister's *inspiring* eulogy, on the other hand, revealed evidence of the relief, comfort, and peace that evolves from placing one's total trust in God's divine providence. She described the broad community involvement of family, friends, and neighbors that supported their loved ones through eighteen months of trauma. Opening arms to future offers of assistance, she reminded survivors, will lighten the load of the difficult journey ahead.

At the conclusion of this admirable woman's funeral, relatives and friends greeted one another, *relieved* that loving connection comforted their aching hearts. Through empathetic sharing at this emotionally charged service, all present were sustained, rejuvenated, and filled with hope, much the same as a climber preparing to ascend Mount Rainier.

In reflection, one is *grateful* for having been a part of Patty's terminal illness journey; for the moments of serious discussions, especially on topics of faith; for sharing gleeful times with her children; and for the ability to serve the family during her final months of life. As the hiker relishes the challenging climb, people learn to treasure significant connections with other human beings. Humbly being open to these interactions enhances one's travels, a single peak or valley at a time.

In the beginning, a mother experiences these eight feelings in giving joyful birth to her newborn. In the end, family and friends encounter them once again through the process of sorrowful love and tender remembrance at the passing of a loved one.

Describe a traumatic event you experienced.

What or who helps you through challenging periods?

My Blankee

Until recently, I believed the relationship with my laptop to be of the love-hate variety. Loving it for its capability to create documents, while shifting words and paragraphs around like figures on a chessboard. Hating it when *it* deleted information, contracted a virus, and slowed down to a snail's pace!

Twice within the same day, I met two business employees expressing similar frustrations, and both with that same angry, my-life-is-out-of-control demeanor. *Oh,* I thought, *so I'm not the only one who allows a machine to take charge of my emotions.*

In the past, when taking my laptop in for observation and technical assistance, I stressed myself into a tether, as if the end of the planet may occur if the machine didn't get fixed TODAY. Donning my power dressing, dress for success clothes, I traveled to the store from which I purchased the machine and warranty plan. I approached the counter, using self-talk to convince myself that I could handle this tech stuff all by myself.

The technician, who treated me with understanding and patience, must have wondered about my obvious sense of frustration, limited computer knowledge, and fear of unknown territory. Conversely, I thought, *How could this twenty-something young man, who experienced a technology-integrated elementary and secondary education, possibly understand my discomfort?* Fortunate for the younger generation, being raised in a computer world allowed for quick learning and natural comfort with a computer, similar to learning skiing and swimming at an early age.

Handing over the laptop for a two-to-five week repair job felt similar to a child giving up his favorite "blankee." To some children, the blanket, a sense of emotional security and warmth, serves as a best friend and constant companion. Without a doubt, a significant number of parents, I am certain, recall waiting until their child fell asleep before quietly reaching into the crib and slipping the blanket from under the toddler's head. With expediency, the mom or dad then made trips with the blankee to the washer and then the dryer, hoping that the treasured item dried before the child awakened. A toddler without his security blanket is not a happy camper!

My laptop, *my* blankee, serves as a useful tool for writing, recording important data, and searching for needed information. How could I possibly live without it for an extended period of time? Why am I allowing it to control my feelings, thoughts, and actions?

As a young child matures, she or he outgrows the need for a beloved blanket. In an effort to follow this same pattern, I began to perceive my laptop as a tool, a machine that sometimes requires repair. Being a *thing,* I put its importance in my life in perspective, not allowing it to control me.

Before my last visit to the computer store, I decided to try using a sense of humor and a positive attitude. Likewise, I dressed for inner success by focusing on a calm demeanor, allowing ample time for the diagnosis of the machine's current symptoms, arriving early in the morning, and taking lots of deep breaths during the process. I stood near the service desk, smiled, and asked, "Is the Computer Doctor in?" The pleasant technician returned the smile and I immediately felt a win-win relationship envelop my spirit. In a relaxed manner, we discussed the current symptoms of the *thing,* and explored possible repair strategies.

Having a computer, I concluded, is parallel to owning a house. Each continues to be a "work-in-progress." Periodically, things need fixing. That's just the way it is. And as I work through each observation and repair process, I learn something new about the *thing* and about myself. Using this situational psychology theory seems to give purpose and meaning to the experience.

My laptop remains a necessary piece of equipment – and as such requires periodic check-ups, new updates, and sometimes repairs. As of this writing, my laptop needs to visit the repair shop again. Truth be known, I'm going to miss my blankee.

Explore thoughts about a thing that can be a source of frustration.

What strategies assist you in giving proper perspective to your thoughts, feelings, and actions regarding it?

Near Fatal Experiences

Three times before the age of eleven, traumatic experiences nearly ended my young life. Why not? One must await the answer to such a question, as only the Master Planner's reflections can shed light upon these "Why me? Why not me?" puzzling thoughts.

When I was age three, my mother dressed me in a bright red, thick snowsuit, as well as hat and gloves, in preparation for a trip with my father on a bitterly cold winter day. Snowbanks lined the country road as we traveled to visit local ranchers. Driving south on the homebound trip, I recall standing on the rear floor of the car and holding on to the front seat – seatbelts not yet invented – and chatting with Dad. Suddenly, I fell to the right, hitting the handlebar, causing the door to open. Out I toppled, rolling and rolling until coming to an abrupt halt. Dad stopped the car, and rushed to scoop me up off the gravel road. Poor Dad. He must have been so frightened of what he might find! Miraculously, being bundled up in the protective snow gear, as well as Dad's traveling at a safe speed, saved my life.

When I was age four, my father drove sixty miles, taking his children on our annual swimming outing. The huge indoor, mineral pool housed both a baby pool and a deeper pool with long slide, gymnastic rings, and nonstop noise from excited swimmers. Strategically placing me in the shallow pool for splashing and dog paddling, my siblings left me to frolic about while they swam in the larger pool. Unfortunately, or perhaps fortunately, the two pools were connected with only a short concrete wall in between. Hopping up and down, I accidentally slithered over the barrier, landing headfirst into the deep pool. Thankfully, my brother John witnessed the split-second fall, and quickly snatched me from the deep water. This frightening incident, along with infrequent opportunities to swim, seemed to implant an early fear of water, resulting in my lack of confidence with water activities.

The pasture behind our country home became the scene of the third near-fatal experience. This acreage, used frequently for wintertime skiing, sledding, and tobogganing, also constituted an area for horseback riding and walks to the hilly acres covered with cedars, wildflowers, and unusual rock formations. Early on, Dad taught me how to feed, water, and groom the horses, put on a bridle and saddle, and to ride. Dolly, my favorite gray mare, seemed especially gentle and receptive to frequent outings. On one occasion, though, at about age eleven, I prepared Dolly for a Sunday afternoon ride into the pasture. Galloping down toboggan hill, so named by the siblings for its deep jump that made for a fast start, Dolly suddenly came to an unexpected stop as we approached this tricky-to-maneuver area. Prior to this sudden move, the saddle had been jostling from side to side, a result of my not cinching the saddle tightly enough. Off I flew through the air, landing hard upon the ground. Badly shaken, but with layers of young adolescent fat to protect my bones, I got up, brushed myself off, and proceeded to walk down the steep toboggan hill, leading Dolly by the reins. I arrived home to find Dad awaiting my return. Maybe parental intuition told him something had gone awry. In his patient, reassuring manner he talked with me about the frightening experience, and suggested strategies for preventing a repeat performance.

Why did I live through these traumatic incidents? Someday, I will know why it was not "my time." Often, we are unaware of close calls with death, as in a near-missed car accident, airplane mishap, terrorist attacks, or tsunami tragedy. Realizing this fact sears upon the mind the importance of living each day as if it were our last, saying our "I love you's," and having our affairs in order, thus remaining prepared for that unknown transition into eternity.

Recall some of your near fatal experiences.

Who helped you through these traumatic events?

What life lessons did you learn as a result of the incidents?

Positive and Flexible

For years, my colleague Julie and I resorted to using the mantra, "Positive and Flexible," as a survival tool. As school counselors, we daily assisted young adults in dealing with life. Each day offered new cases of change and loss issues, academic concerns, parental challenges, child abuse, or suicide threats. To get through the day's work, one crisis after another, we would go into an office, close the door, twirl our index fingers into the air, smile broadly, and chant, "Positive and Flexible!" Almost instantly, the brief sabbatical relieved our tension and rejuvenated us with energy and calm confidence to bravely face waiting clients.

One spring afternoon, however, we had a particularly curious case. A student came crawling on her hands and knees through the media center while angrily oinking like a pig! We looked at each other, both wondering, *Now what do we do?* Quickly, we ushered, or rather coached the girl into an office and began calmly engaging her in dialogue. Unable to reach her parents, we spent a lengthy counseling session together. Gradually, she began to relax enough to complete the school day under our care.

Weeks later, on the last day of school, this same young adolescent ran through the spacious commons area, swinging her heavy bookbag around her head, screaming, "No more stupid school!" As a relief to the student, and to us, the school year had ended at last!

Calm, supportive, trained counselors, coupled with a relaxed office setting, tempered the girl's agitated, angry demeanor. But periodically renewing our own spirits through our "Positive and Flexible" attitude-change stretched our ability to work successfully through this case and numerous others.

Years later, chanting the mantra remains an effective, humorous technique for softening a tense situation and putting a much-needed smile on the face!

Recall a unique situation in which your calm response diffused a possible crisis.

Describe a relaxed, nurturing, ideal setting in your home or workplace.

Simply Live

From whence cometh this desire to live simply, and thereby simply live? As children, we lived quite frugally with Mom and Dad teaching us skills for survival. Rarely did we eat in restaurants, making nutritious meals at home; or go to movies, creating our own entertainment. We learned to sew and mend our own clothes; plant and care for a garden; feed chickens and milk cows. Compensation for helping in the family store consisted of future tuition payments for our higher education.

Early years of my marriage equated to saving money, and accounting for every dime spent. Only after those first fifteen years of single-income living did two incomes relax the financial strain, allowing us to afford a few luxuries. Most of the extras, though, came after sons completed four years of college. Then, it became easier to fall into the materialism trap, collecting far more than needed.

After reading several resources about living a simple life and dealing with household clutter, I began to realize that more "stuff" does not promote good health or happiness. Gradually, I began sorting through and organizing the "stuff." After frequent visits to deposit unwanted and unnecessary items, employees of not-for-profit stores became familiar faces. An interesting observation began to take shape. Never once did I have a moment of regret, even after leaving behind a winter coat with a mink collar that, by the way, had not been worn in twenty years. No, actually, the mental load felt so much lighter. Too many things, it seems, tend to weigh us down, becoming burdensome.

Giving away personal treasures to family and friends elicited a distinct feeling of joy. Without exception, these special individuals accepted them with grateful smiles and open arms. Sharing one's collected memorabilia, useful articles, and clothes touches the giver's heart most deeply. Why keep "stuff" that one no longer has need for and which others might use?

True, citizens need to keep the economy moving forward, the money in circulation. Could it be a matter of balance between need and want; between the haves helping the have-nots; between materialism and philanthropy; between caring for ourselves as well as giving time and energy to others?

Striving to simply live has opened up time for other interests besides shopping; fostered a joyful spirit in giving to others; made for fewer items to clean, repair or for which to find space. Now when I purchase a new item, I give away a similar one. A new book translates into donating a previously used one to the library; a new sweater means giving a gently used one to a person in need.

Part of feng shui theory includes creating a healthy energy flow throughout one's living space. Positioning furniture and wall décor, as well as house location, is all part of this study. Getting rid of clutter promotes positive air circulation. This flow of energy makes for healthier, more peace-filled residents of any living environment, whether home or work related.

Is life beginning to complete a circle? Am I returning to childhood values of conservatism, sharing, and placing more importance on relationships? Formerly, it seemed to me a matter of being born at a time when the Depression after-shock still sent tidal waves of caution through survivors. Currently, however, it feels *right*, as if living simply and serving others are focal points in living well.

Ponder your values and beliefs about living simply.

Describe your efforts to simply live.

Six Who Touched My Life

One of my earliest recollections is that of standing, at age three, near a fence by our family-owned store. A hole beneath the fence, probably dug by one of our pet dogs, provided space through which to crawl. Almost daily, I would wait in that spot calling, "Milton, come get me!" and wait for the elderly gentleman to walk across the street to fetch me. A confirmed bachelor, *Milton* owned a tiny store – similar to a miniature 7-Eleven – in which, among other items, he sold sugar cones filled with generous mounds of delicious, creamy ice cream. Milton, a dear man, helped me feel, at that young age, uniquely special. He not only catered to our hand-holding walk across the street to select my desired flavor of ice cream, but also named his establishment after the two of us. On the roof of his small store, he painted in large white letters: *M & M* for Milton and Meg.

In my late teens, I met a gentleman, *Jonathan*, who treated me with love, kindness, and respect. Dancing together, spending hours in engaging conversation, and playing board games created cherished memories. Kindness, patience, and generosity modeled in a male friend at that early dating age made an indelible, lifelong impression upon me.

A pen pal during my last year of elementary school influenced a critical direction in my educational future. Coincidentally, the same order of Sisters that taught at my grade school also staffed a high school at their Mother House. As a writing assignment, they assigned pen pals to both schools. Actually, this also turned out to be an effective marketing strategy! *Karina*, a student at the Nebraska boarding school, wrote me frequently about her life at the all-girls establishment. Her enthusiasm and personal invitation to attend the same high school significantly encouraged the setting for my secondary education. With my parents' goal to help provide a college education for their seven children, it became a financial stretch to send me to this fine school. However, like developing a taste for Austrian apple strudel or Hawaiian Kona coffee, Karina's letters nurtured my interest, and encouraged the pursuit of my promoting this choice to Mom and Dad. Today, Karina remains a model for personally engaging with other people and caring for their needs.

Sister Hildegarde, a college professor, focused on traditional beliefs about marriage in her classes: man as head of the household; woman's place in the kitchen. However, after being married a few years, I wondered, *What knowledge did she have of dominance and control? Of loss of personal identity as the wife remained home doing household chores and rearing kids?* Arguably, with traditional marriage beliefs taught through church and school at that time, it took years for me to break out of the archaic mold, discovering once again the core of who I am as a person. Gradually, I began to make changes as an individual, wife, and mother. God bless Sister Hildegarde. She meant well.

For thirty years, *Sarah,* my dear friend and mentor, has counseled thousands of elementary school students and hundreds of staff members and parents. Both on and off the job, "Be Kind" remains her rule for living life. Sarah has been known to collect used clothing for the disadvantaged, assist total strangers, and care untiringly for her aging parents. Although conservative by nature, she generously provides people with nutritious meals and oftentimes brings them artistically wrapped presents. As her measure for living life, she makes decisions using the guide, "I've got to be able to look myself in the mirror every day. Will this choice allow me to do so?"

Three years ago, a gentle, petite, and energetic woman introduced me to the contemplative arts. This non-denominational, meditative practice of silently spending time with God has provided daily peace and direction for me, significantly enhancing my life. Even though in her eighth decade of life, *Sister Marie Louisa* still volunteers daily. In serving God through others, she models one of the secrets of a long, happy journey. Someday, the "thief in the night" may have to run a record-setting marathon to catch up with her!

As my paths crossed with these six individuals, we shared a part of life together, created memories, and comforted one another during sorrowful periods. I am grateful that they expressed kindheartedness, assisted me in exploring different values and beliefs, personally engaged themselves in my life, and helped me feel special. I laud them for their patience, perseverance, and tenacity with their own life-issues.

Like the plus and minus ends of a battery, our lives, through relationships, are connected either positively or negatively. When together, people sometimes create a positive flow of energy; at other times, unsettling feelings occur. For me, the positive connections with these six human beings resulted in a significant, heart-warming current.

Write about six people, who are not relatives, whom you respect and admire.

How did experiences with your selected six persons influence your life?

Something I Concentrated On as a Child

Something I concentrated on as a child was music: primarily singing or playing the piano, organ, and accordion, as well as minor experiences with the clarinet, saxophone, and trumpet. My very favorite musical endeavor, though, became singing at church; singing to my dad's piano accompaniment; taking singing lessons during my college days; being part of the school's chorus and stage productions; and as a soloist at weddings.

One of my fondest memories is singing to Dad's accompaniment as he played Schubert's "Ave Maria," the "Cradle Song," and "Too-Ra-Loo-Ra-Loo-Ral," more commonly known as "That's An Irish Lullaby." His mother, both artistically and musically gifted, taught him to play the piano. Dad loved his music, finding it both enjoyable and a challenge.

As I hustled to care for three toddlers, Dad used to tell me, "Keep playing the piano and singing." To date, not doing so has been one of my deepest regrets. On the other hand, it's never too late to begin anew.

Singing, I believe, brings joy to the heart. As one concentrates on the music, making a concerted effort to sound each note perfectly, it becomes a relaxing stress-reducer. So, why am I not nurturing this dormant talent? With grown children, there really is no excuse for not pursuing music interests. At this season of life, it feels fitting to join the church choir or a chorale, affording the opportunity to meet new people and sing beautiful music.

Perhaps, this year, I will sing again.

Describe a favorite childhood activity.

What are you doing now to capture that same joy?

The Coveted Award

Late last night, I received a call from a new friend. The usual daily chitchat behind us, she queried, "Did you really attend a liberal arts college?"

"Yes, I did," I answered proudly.

"Wow! You mean you took all those math, science, language, history, composition and literature, music, art, drama, theology, psychology, and education courses?"

Recalling the four-year experience, I replied, "Yes, I remember spending many hours in the campus library as well as the biology and chemistry laboratories completing assignments."

"Gee, you received a phenomenal education," she deducted.

"I know," I agreed.

When we finished our conversation, I lay awake thinking about how many more ways my undergraduate education stacked up as being liberal. For example, as students we received liberal opportunities to learn proper etiquette. At this Kansas all-girls college, we ate our evening meals in a formal dining room, taking turns serving each other. As a "waitress" we learned when to serve on the left, and when to serve on the right. As a "guest," we learned where to place our eating utensils so that the "waitress" knew when to remove the plate (from the left, of course). With liberal amounts of food served at breakfast, lunch, and dinner, we acquired chubby checks and a liberal expansion of the waistline during those years.

Another part of our liberal education included responsibly caring for ourselves. To the nuns, this meant signing in and out of a log book when we left campus, heeding to the 9:00 p.m. deadline to return to the residence hall each weekday, and securing written parental permission to spend the weekend with another girl's family. Also, without realizing it, the professors gave us a liberal rule associated with wearing caps and gowns to daily church service. Students who overslept just rolled up their pajama bottoms underneath the black robes, which liberally covered the sleepwear!

Learning proper posture included classes with a certain sit-straight-and-tall professor. Picture a freshmen class (with green beanies to designate their low totem-pole status) being instructed to stand with backs straight against the wall: heels, hind ends, shoulders, and heads touching the wall while tummies were sucked in so tightly that they, too, almost touched the wall. Looking directly ahead, our group must have resembled one of those boot camp scenarios. Then, she marched us one by one to the stairwell and, with liberal detail, instructed us in the proper way to both ascend and descend stairs. Having all her minute details ironed into our brains, we graciously could have crashed a debutante ball.

As an incentive to liberally incorporate proper sit-stand-and-walk social graces into a daily habit, the astute professor strategically placed a Posture Award plaque in the hallway of the main campus building. Each semester students who successfully mastered these skills and used them to near perfection had their name added to the plaque. Guess what? I won that coveted award!

Now you might say, "Big whoopee." But, who knows, maybe using proper posture has kept me from having rounded shoulders or osteoporosis, and strengthened my spine. One never knows what long-lasting effects our generously liberal education might provide! My higher education institution included a liberal education of the mind, body, spirit, and social graces. Only one major category was absent – a liberal association with and knowledge about *men*.

What educational experiences did you receive in school besides those taught in the formal classroom?

Which lessons learned during your formal schooling continue to assist you with your life journey?

The Dreaded Envelope

The instant a twelve-year-old girl closed my counseling office door behind her and nervously sat down, I knew a crisis story would soon unfold. When she cast her eyes downward, I was certain of it. Cautiously, she proceeded to tell me about the visits to her grandparents' home within the past year, and the unsolicited touching of her private body parts.

After empathetically listening to her, I clearly explained the law regarding this type of behavior, and my mandated obligation to report it. Gently, I talked about the steps taken by community agencies to protect the alleged victim. When she understood the process and my commitment to assist her through the stages, I telephoned her parents and reported the incidents to the appropriate agency.

Weeks later, I was issued a subpoena for the upcoming preliminary trial. Receiving those dreaded envelopes and the subsequent questioning on a witness stand comprised some of my most challenging responsibilities as a counselor. Following cubs into their den appeared more inviting than participating in a courtroom hearing with alleged perpetrator, defendant, lawyers, witnesses, and jury!

The defense attorney called me after our court session with the news that the grandfather changed his "not guilty" plea to "guilty." Sharing the final verdict and court's sentence with the girl brought tears of relief. With additional community and family assistance, she managed to pace herself through a traumatic event in her life.

As the mother bear protects her cubs, so, too, relatives, friends, and school personnel avail themselves to children's care. In private sessions and in classroom presentations, I encouraged students to tell someone whom they trust if a person is hurting them or making them feel uncomfortable. But, frequently, they reported to me, "They won't believe me. They'll think it's my fault. They won't understand. They don't have time to listen to me."

As caregivers of world youth, it becomes every adult's responsibility to watch over growing children. Through our words and actions, they readily discern whether we – the adults – can be trusted. With available community resources, the world *can* become safer. Even if it means receiving one of those notorious envelopes from the court system, we will know that we made a difference in one child's journey. When and if the occasion arises, we *will* survive courthouse duty, unlike an adventure into a mother bear's den.

Recall an uncomfortable childhood experience.

In what ways have you worked through the trauma?

The Entrance

As I was strolling up the flagstone walkway, my initial glance revealed an entrance that appeared gigantic! With stained glass inserts on each side, the twin burgundy doors created a warm effect for those viewing the massive entrance for the first time. Next to the doorway hung a grapevine wreath intrinsically adorned with dried pink roses and delicate lavender. Gracefully, the wreath softened the mansion-like feel of the main entrance.

Venturing stealthily through the opened doors, I experienced a breathtaking view. Directly ahead, through a horizontal wall of windows, I observed a landscaped garden of rose bushes, fountains spraying water high into the air, and angel figures adorning the natural stone pathway. Offering a cozy ambience, this inspiring, picturesque garden setting complemented the spacious rooms, high vaulted ceilings, and huge entrance.

Within seconds, I heard excited voices from deep within the garden. "Grandma! Grandma! You're here." Running to throw their arms around me, the grandchildren hugged me tightly, making me feel that I *was* in a nurturing, people-loving home, not a chilly castle; a home of love and beauty, not a showplace with a large, architecturally unusual entrance. In reality, this expansive home requires a large doorway, making room for the generous hearts of the welcoming hostess, host, and children who exhibit genuine warmth and love for their guests.

But no matter the size of living quarters, loving people living within any homey residence can treat guests with respect, love, laughter, and relaxed joy. Truth is, as the children's great-grandmother frequently declared, "It takes a lot of living and happy experiences to make a house a home – to put a halo over its roof." Whether a camping tent, homeless shelter, trailer, apartment, condo, or house, by wearing halos of patience and kindness, all people within any living area can feel welcomed, respected, and safe.

Describe living quarters in which you feel welcome and comfortable.

What makes this area different from others?

The Mallard Duck Theory

Marriage, traveling the life journey together, is similar to living like a pair of mallard ducks. As they fly close to a pond, the birds are totally carefree in their approach, flying in circles, but with tunnel vision aimed at just the right landing. This is much the same as a couple's wedding and *honeymoon* stage: blindly in love, focused on celebrating their vows with family and friends, then living their future moments together with eager joy and acceptance of the unknown future. Ducks, too, come in for that landing, anticipating food, rest, and frolicking fun in the water.

While sitting on a wharf recently, I noticed how the ducks swam to one location, then another, wherever there seemed to be hope of nourishment. Some even flew from the water on to the boarded area, strutting to within an arm's reach. With a mission in mind and hungry stomachs, they didn't appear to be shy. The *industrial* stage of marriage seems to be likewise so. Couples eagerly establish roots, care for family and the community, and proceed forward with their careers, as well as individual and common goals. The tunnel vision of the initial stage remains, but the focus is now changed.

Like the pair of mallard ducks, a couple uses currents to maneuver through the rhythms of life. Most noticeably, the ducks gliding downstream seem to alter the leadership position. So, too, in marriage, two individuals discover their talents, gifts, and needs and glide through life as partners, yet altering leadership roles as they use their unique strengths. Marriage becomes a partnership of give and take, of sensing one another's needs, of traveling the journey like the skilled, determined pair of ducks. Riding the current through the rocks, around branches and debris, the ducks keep traveling forward, just like people working through the hiccups of life.

Once in a while, ducks swim the waters alone, but typically they gather as a unit. Maybe they, too, understand the value of caring, kindness, and compassion, especially as the growing-up years take couples into the *rest and renewal* stage of their marriage. Life's rhythm has slowed, but the physical and emotional needs still provide abundant opportunities for family and community members to assist in this spiritually invigorating stage. This autumn of life – reaping value from life experiences, lessened family responsibilities, and with, hopefully, the comforts of life provided – remains a time to explore new interests, discover hibernated talents, and travel to new frontiers.

One of my favorite duck views is that of watching them glide in for a water landing. Like children playing follow-the-leader or sky divers approaching an earthly touchdown, they seem to target a spot, throttle their jets, hit just right, and skim across the bay, leaving a ripple pattern behind. Each time, the landing seems near perfect. When a couple retires, they, too, put the skids on their formerly busy, sometimes hectic, lifestyles. With major responsibilities completed, they now are free to pursue other interests at a slower pace, health and finances permitting, before the onset of the *reflective* stage. This final period of their journey may find them spending much more time at home, dependent on the assistance of caregivers and medical personnel.

The honeymoon, industrial, rest and renewal, and reflective stages of marriage offer countless opportunities for personal growth. In thinking about maneuvering through the valleys and peaks of life, I am reminded of a plaque that my dad kept readily visible in his workshop. It read: "Train your mind by persistent effort to take life slowly. Keep in low gear the whole day long no matter what happens." (author unknown) My wise father understood the importance of mind, body, and spirit balance. Perhaps his navigational tool might serve us well as we progress through the different stages of marriage. In so doing, we, like the mallard ducks, can glide through life, take one valuable second at a time, and enjoy the flight.

Describe your analogy of marriage.

What strategies assist you in being part of a relationship?

The Perfect Tree

In reflecting upon the ambitious, nerve-testing building of a house, I recall the trauma that accompanied *the perfect tree*. Apprehensive of the contractor's forty-foot-at-maturity conifer choices for a small patio home yard, I set about searching for the perfect tree. Telephone conversations and visitations to local nurseries, Internet research, and exploration with city officials led to a proposed choice, which, by the way, required builder approval. After numerous memos and discussions with decision-making personnel, the landscape company received permission for the purchase and planting of a Columnar Norwegian Spruce tree.

The cordial, accommodating owner of the landscape company searched city-wide until he located this challenging-to-find tree. Once delivered, however, we could not yet celebrate, as the perfect location for the perfect tree needed to be selected. Being a visual learner, I sweetly, pleadingly asked the landscaper – still cordial and accommodating, I might add – to move this large balled tree to three different locations before announcing, "Okay, that's the perfect spot."

Laboriously digging just the right size hole and filling it with quality soil mixture, the patient, foreign-speaking laborers dropped the heavy load into the designated spot, filled the hole, crowned it with decorative wood bark, and steadied the tree with two sturdy poles for erect growth. *Ah*, I thought. *The perfect tree, the perfect site!*

But, wait, the saga continues. On the empty lot bordering this unique spruce was soon to be built another house, with its sidewalk only a few feet from the tree. Now completed, the neighboring house shades the spruce tree, limiting its sunlight. Also, two houses within ten feet of one another squelch the once spectacular view of the perfect tree – different from any of the other surrounding eighty residences. Admittedly, the perfect tree is still perfect in stature, but not with the "Wow!" effect for which I so diligently planned.

The whole incident served to remind me once again that the world isn't perfect, nor is any human being, creature, or situation. From whence, then, comes this drive to be perfect? My father used to remark that predictably I strived to be the best – perhaps due, in part, to my mother's modeling. She taught me, for example, that every sewing, crochet, or knitting stitch had to be perfect, or ripped out and completed all over again. Also, as a large, conservative family, we had many blessings, but were, by no means, materially affluent. Hence, we were taught to care for our necessary possessions meticulously.

Mother used to tell the story of getting me ready to go to one of her club meetings. One day, I overheard my Mom lamenting to her friends, "In preparing to leave home, I have to allow extra time to clean up both her *and* her doll!"

Before each trip, I pleaded, "Mama, will you wash and iron Geraldine's clothes before we go?" Poor Mom. She already had enough laundry with nine people in the family. Nevertheless, she honored my request in order that I might take with me the perfectly dressed doll. Mother also told the story of my maternal grandfather, Luke, who kept his blacksmith shop and tools perfectly clean and in perfect order. Did she, then, come by this familial characteristic vicariously?

Striving to get the best grades in school, then to be a supermom and the best school counselor in my career made being a recovering perfectionist challenging. Several of my middle school counselees who, feeling compelled by parents to excel not only in school but also in extracurricular activities, threatened to commit suicide. The drive to please and to stretch beyond healthy limits left them feeling desperate, hopeless, and wanting to give up life's journey. Perfectionism, I have learned, is a characteristic to be respected and dealt with, as it may have stormy repercussions.

Like *the perfect tree* settled into its carefully selected location, we, too, are meant to grow, to become, to inspire – but as physically, mentally, spiritually, and emotionally balanced beings. Granted, the centered self is different for each person, creating the necessity of establishing one's own well-being baseline. The body gives us signals when it is feeling out of balance and, like the Columnar Norwegian Spruce, needing more sunshine and nourishment laced with tender loving care. Responding to these messages becomes essential to our physical, mental, and spiritual health.

Living responsibly, we have but to listen, to pay heed, to periodically tweak our expectations and lifestyles. In so doing, we will lead not perfect, but healthier, happier, more peaceful lives. Attaining perfection, much the same as looking for that pot of gold at the end of a rainbow, is not a human possibility. So, let's stretch for excellence, learn to massage the aching muscles of disappointment with a sense of humor, and move onward.

Describe a time when your push to excel became a challenge to yourself or to others.

Which implemented strategies help you to feel centered?

The Self

Being reared on a Native American Reservation near the serene Badlands of South Dakota by a calm, nurturing yet humorous father helped shape my *caring self*. In this peaceful part of our great United States, my father never passed up an opportunity to be warm and cordial to others and to assist those in need. One day, I recall accompanying him to visit an elderly Lakota woman, Lillian, who lay ill on her single bed in a one-room, dirt-floor home. Dad brought her a large brown bag filled with groceries, his smile, and comforting words. His modeling, as well as my early childhood experiences of living as a minority, taught me to accept others as they are, as well as to appreciate diversity.

My mother, a talented and devoted homemaker, nurtured my *creative self* by allowing me to learn, under her guidance, the art of cooking, sewing, gardening, and different crafts. My father played the piano every day and encouraged my musical talent through piano, vocal, organ, and accordion lessons. Each morning, as mother prepared breakfast, Dad played Chopin's Nocturne in E Flat on the piano, exemplifying the importance of continual practice of one's talents.

My twenty-two years in the field of school counseling deeply impressed upon me the need for a positive family life. Hence, my resolved determination to be an important part of my children and grandchildren's villages. Aware of young adults longing for someone to listen to them, to do things with them, and to feel their loneliness made me determined and committed to providing a better life for children. In so doing, my caring self continues to be stimulated as

I share creative experiences with them, nurturing and encouraging the development of their own unique selves.

Describe your caring and creative selves.

In which ways do they continue to be nurtured and "grow?"

The Village Spirit

On a recent trip to Cape Breton, Nova Scotia, the village concept became more real as I observed community inhabitants joining together to support one another. While not anxious to drive on an unknown road and through night fog to reach the Normandy Inn, I left early, as advised by the Visitor Center, in order to arrive in ample time to claim a chair in "The Barn." On a Saturday night in early October, community and visitors alike arrived for a Ceilidh (pronounced "kaylee," meaning "gathering"), a traditional coming together to enjoy fiddling, piano playing, and stepdancing. For hundreds of years, the Cape Bretoners have kept alive the Celtic music of their ancestors. But it isn't just the music and dancing that makes this custom unique. It's the village support that mushrooms from these gatherings. Steady, constant, and dependable. The community camaraderie is always there, like the endless flow of the Margaree River, or Beulah Falls in Cape Breton National Park.

Stars shining around the harvest moon became nature's desktop wallpaper for this structure known as "The Barn," obviously a former livestock building converted into a community gathering place for performances and square dancing. Soon all the chairs filled with folks greeting one another. The musicians tuned their fiddles to exact pitch, looking around for their piano accompanist. Whew! Arriving one minute before curtain time, she sat on the piano bench and nodded to the emcee that the show could begin.

Now, the master of ceremonies, presumably the owner of "The Barn," became a curious study. With a toddler on top of his shoulders and microphone in hand, he introduced the musicians, engaged the audience in dialogue at various points, and exhibited warmth and concern for the community members. Sometimes he switched toddlers, and soon it became obvious that he had both a young son and daughter. At various intervals, they, too, walked about the stage, held an old violin with one string, or chatted into a toy microphone. Sometimes, community members coached them to sit on their laps.

The musicians and talented artists delighted everyone by untiringly playing the fast tempo Celtic music and performing step dance routines. Clapping and stomping feet, the audience both encouraged and congratulated the musicians showing their support for keeping the tradition alive. Even audience members were invited to dance and play the piano. A fishing guide from Maine strummed his guitar, engaging the audience in singing with him. The whole evening's entertainment resulted in a real community event!

Two hours of a lively performance followed by additional hours of square dancing provided a golden opportunity for community involvement. The entire evening reminded me of community square dancing, card playing, branding cattle, picnics, and rodeos I had experienced growing up in a small South Dakota village. During these similar get-togethers, people gathered to have fun, physically assist one another, and celebrate living. With varied age groups, the younger generation learned to model the activities of their elders, and to feel support in their endeavors.

On branding days, the cowboys arrived to help one another brand the cattle; women, typically, cooked a bountiful feast. Naturally, the ladies enjoyed catching up on news as they prepared mounds of potato salad, coleslaw, fried chicken, biscuits, and lots of pies. When the hard-working cowboys took a break at mid-day, women, men, and children all sat down for nourishment and more visiting. As a young child, I sneaked out in the afternoon to watch the branding process. Seeing the calf on the ground, hearing its painful cries, and smelling the burning hide as the branding iron left its mark, sent me quickly to a play area, never to return to the action setting again.

Where do we find this important village concept now? I asked myself. Unless created, the occasions for community affairs do not seem to occur as frequently as in former days. Nevertheless, the need to belong, to feel an important part of the family and village is of paramount importance to living an emotionally healthy life. Perhaps there *are* existing opportunities awaiting our involvement. If so, joining in with the work and fun needs to become a priority, resulting in heaps of nurturing and encouraging support.

Where have you discovered the important village concept in your life?

In which community activities do you feel supported?

Tight Fist, Tight Heart

oney, it seems, generates a myriad of feelings, both positive and negative. Having begging children follow with outstretched hand in Tunisia, Africa, and Ocho Rios, Jamaica, arouses something deep within my heart, a lasting reminder that two-thirds of the world's population goes to bed hungry every night. Monetary poverty surrounded me and tugged at my heart the first twenty-one years of my life, during which I lived on a Native American reservation. Although my experiences are not all-encompassing, my travels to twenty-three foreign countries, five Canadian provinces, and forty-six states in North America allowed occasions to witness physical results from the lack of money in the eyes of Africans, Jamaicans, Asians, and the Lakota Sioux. But physical poverty does not equate with emotional poverty.

As a school counselor, I listened to many emotionally starved young adults sadly relate that they judged their family members as being too busy to listen to them, to do fun things together. Frequently, I encouraged them to schedule a "date" with their parent(s) in order to promote opportunities for open dialogue. Living within a family unit and without feelings and ideas being "heard" leads to lonely isolation. When communication improved at home, I observed more contented, relaxed, and hopeful gazes in the eyes of my counselees. It does not take money to give children time, to share thoughts and feelings, to both work and have fun times together.

As a middle-class person (again, such a relative term) with several decades of life-experience as well as living abroad, I have engaged in varied class-distinction experiences: deeply spiritual burial customs of Native Americans to gala fund-raising dinners attended by generous philanthropists for nonprofit organizations. What were the similarities, the differences? Both, I observed, are locked deep within each person's soul, but take shape in our body language and conversations. For example, the manner in which people greet one another: Is there a genuine, welcome feel to the smile, the bow of the head, the handshake, or does one sense an ulterior motive to the gesture? Are the conversational topics self- or other-focused? Does one offer to assist another person's need only when it is self-serving?

Life's journey has shown me that folks who are generous in kind, compassionate interaction with others and respectful of Mother Earth and all that it offers to its guests, also have a generous monetary spirit. "Spread it ($) around," my Dad used to say in reference to money. By the same token, this quintessential, generous man added this special prayer before each meal blessing: "God, please help us be mindful of the needs of others."

A tightfisted person also seems to have strong, tight cords around the heart, tightly guarding both money and emotions. An open-handed person, by contrast, appears to have a welcoming, kind, and compassionate spirit. Similar to the control on a gas log fireplace, it is within our power to monitor the warmth and beauty of generosity.

I have a friend who carries a penny in her pocket as a way to remember that "In God We Trust." It also serves to prompt her to be mindful of the emotional, spiritual, mental, and physical needs of others. This strategy seems to work well for her, as her heart grows more generous each time she reaches out to help someone.

How do you think someone else would describe your monetary habits?

Describe the character traits of a generous family member or friend.

Too Funny!

ver find yourself experiencing a close call with a near disastrous situation? Maybe frequently? This morning's series of events produced just such an ordeal.

The surrounding setting is a beautiful mountain town with exquisite shops and luxurious accommodations. My fellow conference attendees and I share a spacious, tastefully decorated condo with – get this – four bathrooms and a jacuzzi! It feels like seventy-two hours of living like the rich and famous. The multi-star resort amenities become even more appealing as I experience invigorating walks on the nature trail, and gaze at stellar views of snowy peaks, unusual cloud formations, and autumn aspen leaves.

Upon return from a crisp, thirty-four-degree morning walk, I shared a cup of coffee with condo-mates, then decided to prepare for the morning conference session. My assigned bathroom, decorated in leopard motif, had a glass shower door. With water adjusted to warm temperature, I stepped in, closed the door securely behind me, and proceeded with the usual toiletry. My first inkling that this might be one of those very bad hair days was that, operating on automatic power, I shampooed my hair, then added *styling gel*, assuming it was moisturizer.

So, I started all over again: scrubbing, shampooing and moisturizing, then stepping out of the shower and closing the door behind. All dried off, and ready to put the finishing touches on my hair, I realized the styling gel was still in the shower! I pulled on the shower door, then pulled harder, and even harder on the third try. Still the door would not open. Oh, no! The desperately needed gel for the frizzy, wet hair sat motionless in the shower, innocent of my sudden switch from automatic pilot to panic mode!

Then, the what-if scenarios crept into my brain, like some ghostly vision haunting me. What if I had locked myself in the shower and needed to call for help in my dripping wet birthday suit? What if the maintenance help arrived, trying politely not to look at this mature naked woman staring at them, in utter humiliation, through the glass door?

Later, I thought, *Okay, where's the humor in this? What lesson am I to learn: Don't latch the door when taking a shower? Hang a towel over the door, just in case I can't get out?* The bottom line is, it could have been worse. It really could have happened!

The frizzy hair? No one even commented on it! Each day, it is the unknowns that creep up that keep us looking for creative options – opportunities, if you will – to share even an almost drastically humiliating experience with a sense of humor.

Recall a near disastrous experience.

In reviewing the incident, what humor can you find in it?

Trippin' Out

lessed has been my life journey! Generously, I have been provided with opportunities to see God's creation worldwide. International travel, it seems, has broadened my perspective on life issues, deepened my acceptance of others, and brought me more in touch with different cultures, values, and beliefs. How intriguing it all is: Bavarian Alps of Germany, Norway's fiords, museums in France, Italy's priceless artwork, humble craftspeople of Yugoslavia, the Netherlands' hybrid tulips, Danish pastry in Denmark, Spain's bull fights, begging children in Tunisia, Swiss Alps with grazing cows, Hong Kong's multitudes of people, China's Peking duck, the easy-going lifestyle in Jamaica, sandy beaches of Mexico, Belgium's quaint buildings, the modern art museum in Liechtenstein, Austria's architecture and Tyrolean Alps, ocean views from Nova Scotia's shoreline, New Zealand's fiords and rain forests, and Australia's fairy penguins.

A most frightening as well as embarrassing moment, though, occurred in Germany. After a long day of sightseeing, we started looking for lodging about nine o'clock in the evening. With many tourists attending the Wine Market Fair in Mainz, we had a difficult time finding a place to spend the night. Finally, we located accommodations within close proximity of railroad tracks. The two tiny hotel rooms provided shelter, but proved to be very noisy, with trains frequently passing nearby during the night.

Not wanting the young children to be alone in a room by themselves, I let the five-year old sleep with me in one room and the other two in a separate room with their father at the other end of the hallway. I left my door unlocked just in case my sons from the other room needed me for something. In the middle of the night, a distraught man walked into the room, stood over my nightgown-clad body, and shouted in his native language (which I didn't understand), trying to explain that *he* had paid for this particular room! Finally, he left, shaking his head in frustration, and me shaking, with the sheet tucked tightly under my chin. As a result of that frightening, embarrassing experience, I vowed to always lock hotel room doors.

During "Trippin Out" adventures, I noted that sunrises and sunsets play an important role in a person's daily life cycle. Sunrises recharge my batteries, putting me in high gear for the day ahead. The most memorable sunrise I ever witnessed was in New Brunswick on the Northumberland Strait. I awakened early, ready to start the coffeepot. But when I walked into the living room of the quaint cottage located near the shoreline, I saw the sky ablaze with a spectacular sunrise across the entire horizon. Lone sailboats, docked in the still bay, added to the peaceful scene. Red and orange hues decorated the sky; blue, calm waters of the Strait resisted the gentle disturbance by fishing vessels. I wondered, *Did the fishermen rise early to witness the brilliantly painted sky, the fishing just an excuse to be there in order to capture brief moments of earthly beauty?*

Sunsets put me in low gear for the remaining evening hours, setting the tone for the universe's next rhythmic drama featuring stars, planets, and darkness. Sometimes, as an added gift, the light of the moon generates twilight of spiritual energy enhancing contemplation on the day that is now gone forever, and the hope and trust in tomorrow's gifts and challenges.

When it is time for another Trippin' Out adventure, I pack bags, load up the car, or prepare for the airport shuttle ride, and say to my faithful traveling buddy, "Okay, Jack. It's time to hit the road again."

Share your most frightening or embarrassing travel experience.

What did these experiences teach you for future adventures?

Describe a memorable sunrise or sunset.

What Matters Most

"What do you want your legacy to be? To look like?" asked my financial planner, Lewis.

"What do you want to leave to your children? Your grandchildren? Your community? The world?" he continued.

"Duh," I replied. "I don't have the foggiest idea."

"Well, it's time you started giving these questions some serious consideration – you know, getting your affairs in order," he gently encouraged.

"Oh, that stuff," I responded. "All right. I'll give it some thought," I begrudgingly agreed.

Who wants to think about *not* being here? What do I do with a lifetime of collected items? What to say to family and friends before leaving them behind? As emotionally charged as for any previous task attempted, I forged ahead, striving to give serious planning and organizational strategy to the tedious job.

Now, after two years of sandwiching this effort between selling a home, packing up all belongings, and moving to a different house, I honestly can report to Lewis that my affairs *are* in order – for the most part, that is. The files are relatively clutter-free; finances organized and housed in minimum locations; household extras passed on; and letters of affection and gratitude written to children, grandchildren, and significant friends in my life.

A wise decision to follow the financial planner's directions? *Perhaps yes,* in making the after-a-loss tasks easier for loved ones. *Maybe no,* for it may rob them of the significant, albeit painful, growing experience of sorting through a deceased person's affairs.

Additionally, the multi-year task prevented me from spending more time on what matters most: the legacy I take with me, not the legacy I leave behind. More specifically, what means most to me is taking into eternity a deep faith and love for the Creator, as well as a caring track record of serving others.

From this day forward, I vow to concentrate on each day, each precious moment of traveling the journey with God and my loved ones. The stuff left behind? One lighted match may eliminate responses to the fatiguing question, "What are we going to do with all this stuff?"

What are your goals for this life?

Describe thoughts about your personal legacy.

Part IV

NURTURING THE SPIRIT WITHIN

(Spirituality)

"Peace between countries must rest on the solid foundation
of love between individuals."

Mahatma Gandhi (1869-1948)

A Bar Mitzvah

"Hello," greeted my long lost friend on the phone.

"Well, hi there," I excitedly responded. Although my friend and I were former colleagues, working in adjoining counseling offices, we had not seen each other for three years.

After sharing general updates, she asked, "Would you like to attend my son's bar mitzvah?"

"Yes," I said. Having limited background on this Jewish tradition, I soon realized I had committed to attending an unfamiliar ritual.

A bit nervously, I traveled to the selected destination and entered a church shared by different religions. Family and friends alike gathered to witness this coming-of-age ceremony. The diverse congregation shared their support by taking time to be present for the event and to celebrate afterward with fellowship and refreshments.

In listening to the acquired knowledge shared by Joshua as well as the loving messages of his parents and mentor, I realized the tremendous time, effort, and love that preceded this special day. Hours and hours of study, the parental commitment to a well-schooled son, and the necessary community involvement demonstrated significant dedication to this critical adolescent stage.

After the service, I congratulated Joshua, and commented, "You really worked hard for this special moment."

"Yes, I know," he declared. "But lots of people helped me reach this point."

No matter a person's beliefs or religious preference, we all can live the lyrics to the contemporary song, "We Are Family." Being a part of Joshua's bar mitzvah reminded me of the importance of helping one another from birth to death, and celebrating life events. In like manner, attending this traditional ritual in an ecumenical church setting, with a congregation that was eclectic in age, race, gender, ethnicity, spiritual beliefs, and economic status provided a glimpse of hope for a unified diverse society.

Joshua's generation may be the beginning of an improved era of respectful, accepting human beings. I am grateful that I replied favorably to my friend's invitation and, in so doing, witnessed hope for a hospitable, inter-spiritual, global society.

Describe ways in which an unfamiliar religious event touched your life.

How have various spiritual experiences broadened your knowledge of God or a Higher Power?

An August Reprieve

With trepidation in my heart, I journeyed to a retreat setting I had not yet experienced, a Benedictine Abbey of contemplative nuns in northern Colorado. When making advance reservations, Sister Cecilia said, "Now just keep driving about thirty miles north of Fort Louie until you reach milemarker 381. Then, make an immediate left, going west." I was grateful for her explicit directions, as otherwise I would have found myself in Wyoming.

I also recalled Sister's final advice: "Upon arrival, go to the main Abbey building and ring the doorbell." But after waiting several minutes, I thought perhaps the nuns decided not to open the impressive oak door and admit this little stranger from the big city. Shortly thereafter, a hospitable lady, Sister Josephine, welcomed me into the foyer. Clothed in full habit, Sister was most gracious in presenting her Retreat Center orientation, concluding with the casual comment: "One thing I need to mention is to watch out for rattlesnakes. We've had a lot of rain this year and, consequently, have seen a few of them." *Yikes!* I thought. *Did I really come to an appropriate setting for a quiet time of prayer and meditation?*

An observant walker, I naturally practice being aware of surroundings whether in the city, on the beach, or at an Abbey. Did I need to heed Sister Josephine's warning? Absolutely. However, during my stay neither resident nor guest spotted any of the slithering, rattling, hissing creatures, and they certainly will not deter me from making a future trip to the same location.

After spending two days at the Abbey, I definitely concluded that I *had* come to the right area for peace, reflection, and prayer. Would I return to this retreat setting? Yes, but for a longer period of time. Within one hundred miles of a major city, a person can witness nuns riding tractors, bailing hay, taking care of grazing cows and llamas, managing the well-stocked gift shop, and chanting God's praises during services. (Amazing to learn how speedily they change from work attire to church clothes eight times a day!)

Being in this contemplative setting with its natural beauty of granite formations, wheatfields, wildflowers, native grasses, and Benedictine nuns was an August reprieve for my mind, body, and spirit.

Describe a getaway where you experienced a nurturing of the mind, body, and spirit.

Where do you plan to rendezvous for your next spiritual growth experience?

Anything Will Help

As I celebrate this holiday season in the land of plenty, the issue of materialism surfaces again and again. Each shopping center visit or media advertisement suggests the purchase of the latest technology, expensive jewelry, or most popular toy. How does a person combat consumerism, establish boundaries around gift giving, and define sincere ways to show one's love and concern for others? Finding suitable answers to these questions is not an easy assignment.

Most days when returning home from volunteering at an inner city hospital, I travel the same route. On one street corner stands a homeless gentleman with a sign that reads, "Homeless. Anything will help." A few more details explain his plight in life: Vietnam Vet, U.S. Marine. Usually, I have a little sack of goodies for him – nothing grand, just a few granola bars and fruit. Although the gift is meager, his response is generous. With a smile, he faithfully says, "Thanks so much."

I often wonder about Samuel. *Where does he sleep at night? Where does he get daily food and warm clothes? Who cares for him when he becomes ill?* Given the information on his small sign, it is clear that he served his country, helped secure our freedom and that of others – perhaps even on foreign soil. Although motorists are not privy to his history of becoming homeless, they certainly might assist him and his counterparts while in such a needy state.

In this great nation, many homeless women, children, and men struggle to exist. In our city alone, there are eleven thousand homeless human beings! With assistance, some are able to support themselves once again. Many others, on cold winter days as well as blistering hot summer afternoons, patiently, desperately, and hopefully stand on street corners with their signs.

One need not be rich – another relative term – to be a philanthropist. Sharing of time, talent, and treasure is an opportunity that awaits all humans, albeit in differing degrees. If "anything will help," perhaps we might buy less for ourselves and share more of our abundance with others. In giving to others, hearts become aglow with love.

Carrying a ziplock bag of goodies in the car may be only a small stretch in helping with our nation's homeless, but a recipient who offers a smile and heartfelt "thank-you" certainly appreciates the treats and warms my heart in the brief encounter.

What efforts have you made to monitor materialism in your own life?

What are your values and beliefs about assisting the homeless?

Be Peace

*I*f there is to be peace on this planet, it must begin with me, with my *being* peace. In so doing, this calm countenance will leave a sense of peace with other human beings, similar to the ripples left by a paddling duck initiating flight into the sky. Subsequently, if each person chooses to *be* peace, the aura of kindness and compassion will spread rapidly throughout the world, like an avalanche beginning from a high mountain peak, traveling speedily downward into a river, then forging its way to the open sea.

Now, admittedly, I am not always peace-filled. Before embarking upon a trip, I can be a frenzied lunatic washing clothes, packing, cleaning house (just in case something happens and I don't return home), delegating tasks, and getting affairs in order (again, just in case....). Basically, I become a triple A-type personality whom being around is not pleasant!

To *be* peace requires striving to create a calm environment daily, including periods of trip preparation. Some homes of this multi-task, make-every-moment-count generation, feel like a beehive with the queen bee feverishly directing anxious activity of worker bees. Studies have shown that these worker bees, during strenuous foraging periods, live an average of only four to five weeks. Is there a lesson in the worker bees' lifestyle for us? Will we pay a health price for our scurry-here-and-there lifestyles? I don't know. What I have come to realize, though, is that when my body, mind, and spirit are out-of-sync, I am less at peace; less a *Be* Peace human being; and less physically and emotionally healthy and happy.

If we choose to serve others as a *Be* Peace person, then a soothing mien, like the fragrance of roses, will be passed on to others. Calm demeanor, acceptance of others, and respectful interactions all lend themselves to establishing a peaceful environment. The experience transcends our being, creating a delicate moment that brings a smile to those in our space, as occurs when observing a monarch butterfly flitting from flower to bush.

Where, then, does one find peaceful escapes to maintain a *Be* Peace lifestyle? The choices are varied for uniquely different folks. Personally, I find peace in botanic garden visits, quiet morning walks, meditations in nature, or in the solemnity of churches.

Kindness, compassion, and love of others pave the way for a peaceful existence. As we strive to *be* peace, the spirit of peace will flourish like the springtime spread of dandelions, floating cotton from cottonwood trees, and purple alyssum nourished with rich topsoil and generous water nutrients. In reality, the answers for finding peace and to *be* peace lay within each person's spirit, in dormant repose until the peace-seeker's awakening.

Describe the symptoms of your peaceful versus out-of-sync nature and environment.

Where are your Be Peace escapes?

Create Your Own Day

Being an early riser, I eagerly drove west at 6:30 one summer morning, soon reaching the Rocky Mountain foothills. Blessed with an inch of rain the previous evening, the lush green hills became "alive with the sound of music," as I listened to the gentle wind rhythms, rustling leaves, and chirping birds. A lone deer, with head raised high, like a giraffe munching on tall tree leaves, ate its breakfast from the tippy-top scrub oak bush.

An elderly Capuchin offered Mass in the peaceful chapel. After a hearty breakfast in the community dining room, I climbed the three hundred and seventy-five steps to the mountaintop. Along the way, I paused at each Italian mosaic plaque depicting the Way of the Cross as well as stone shrines portraying each rosary decade. At the summit rests an enormous Sacred Heart of Jesus statue and a significantly smaller one of Saint Mother Cabrini. Surrounding these two figures are fiberglass art pieces representing Moses and the Ten Commandments. Adding a come-here-and-rest feel are several benches, providing comfort while a person absorbs the stellar views of the Continental Divide and cities near the foothills.

Sculpting a peaceful environment for resting with God are shrines, chapels, and walking paths. Adding further to the spiritual ambience are clock chimes echoing through the hills each hour, delicate poppies, low-growing wildflowers, gentle aspens, and sturdy conifers. But there *is* one caveat. If you choose to climb all the steps to the mountaintop, be prepared to experience sore calves the next three days!

Creating a day of spiritual growth at this inspiring location far exceeded my expectations for peace, solace, meditation, writing, and prayer. In truth, the eight-hour getaway scripted a musical composition for the soul.

Within an hour's travel from your home setting, where might you find spiritual renewal?

Discern specific activities that nurture your spirit.

Finding Peace in the Cemetery

There's something about walking in a cemetery that stimulates and massages a peaceful spirit. Step by step, thought after thought, and with each new breath, I pondered life and death issues at each tombstone. In somber ways, cemeteries filled with gravestones well over a hundred years old gently massage thoughts of one's mortality, the brevity of life, and the value of each moment. Century-aged stones; worn inscriptions; foreign languages; the silence; and individual markers adorned with angels, praying hands, lambs, and military insignia elicit a peace-filled environment. In thinking about the finality of this earthly life, I sense a reminder to relax a bit; to remain calm, focused, and at peace. The surroundings serve as evidence that no challenge lasts forever, that life experiences need not result in the loss of a person's mental and spiritual well-being.

While they lived, people beneath these markers may have suffered physical pain as well as emotional trauma. Yet they, too, drew a final breath and transitioned into the next life. Each worked through challenges differently and with varying degrees of familial and community support. If they could speak, would they tell us to travel the journey at a slower pace, to foster healthier relationships, serve others, and to be faithful to God or a Higher Power?

What exactly will those final days, hours, or moments be like? Feel like? Look like? Will it be like closing the eyes and falling asleep at the end of the day? Will I be gasping for air as if nearly drowning in a swimming pool? Will I be angry that my shortened life means that unfinished business will be left behind? Will I be relieved that long days and nights of pain will finally come to an end? Will I, with anticipation, be looking forward to a spiritual existence in the next world?

Not knowing the answers to these questions, I intend to cycle ahead and assist others on their journey as long as I am physically able to do so. Ministering in this way, I expect to be reasonably happy until that final, personal moment. Since ours is a long-distance family, I do not expect loved ones to surround my bedside. In fact, I request anyone who comes to visit me to have a pair of tweezers in her or his pocket and to pluck out any straggling hairs on this woman's chin. Those "whiskers" become more visible when lying flat with face looking upward! I know. Such vanity!

After that final breath, I hope to see white, fluffy clouds as viewed from an airplane thirty-five thousand feet above ground. On many flights, I have noticed these puffy mounds that look like triple-decker ice cream cones softly cuddled together, or like blankets of white cotton candy spread across the horizon. Floating – at least that's what I believe the spirit to do – through the white maze, I'll pass through a welcoming stone archway, and soon thereafter be greeted by God and His heavenly family. Closest to Him will be my son Jerome whom I have waited so long to meet. On each side of him will be my mother and father surrounded by family members and friends.

A surprise element may be added to this glorious occasion. Perhaps the heavenly angels will say, "SURPRISE! Welcome to your homecoming party. Join us for lemon pie, strawberry ice cream, and dark chocolate brownies." They know I can't leave these earthly favorites behind!

Final moments – a cemetery – a peaceful entry into paradise. Such critical concepts to ponder as part of the life-long learning process, bringing a halt, new focus, and then contentment to our hurried selves.

Visit a nearby cemetery.

What life and death thoughts come into your mind?

Consider any changes you may choose to make in your life-journey.

Forgiving Me

One of the most difficult life-lessons is that of self-forgiveness. Learning to deal with issues, putting any residual guilt to the side, and moving on becomes a wearisome trip. On the other hand, not traveling this journey and dwelling on past experiences lead to guilt-ridden periods, which can result in depression.

To suffocate the ugly face of guilt, I attempt to replace each negative thought with a positive one. For example, when recalling the response, "I'm sorry but we can't afford them," to a son who requested to take violin lessons, I concentrate on our multi-country travels while we lived together in Europe. When wishing I could have provided "free rides" for the children's college education, I remember my physical presence at nearly every athletic event and school function.

My many sessions with counselees revealed that giving children too much in the way of materialism could be detrimental to developing a healthy self-concept, and in acquiring confidence and independence. Overall, learning the value of money is an important life skill. Likewise, immediate and extended family members involving themselves in the physical and emotional lives of children is crucial to their early development.

Since we were not born parents, every parent has certain regrets for decisions made regarding the rearing of their children. With one handful of parenting education tidbits and another handful of personal upbringing experiences, personality, and character, adults attempt to parent offspring as best they can. After children are grown, a parent takes time to review previous decisions. Apparent mistakes surface. But it becomes critical, at that time, to learn from the errors and to forgive oneself for any wrongdoing. With a fresh attitude, a parent might concentrate on those positive gifts shared during their children's growing up years, and the successful results of time and effort spent on their behalf.

Statements like "If only I had...." or "Why didn't I...?" may become coarse feed for guilt feelings. Learning from the past and traveling forward, one can make positive changes to lessen the undesirable fodder-growth. In lieu of spending time with non-essential household chores, one might visit a nursing home, call a lonely friend, or baby-sit children of single parents. Truth be known, serving humankind, then, becomes a matter of sharing personal gifts for the betterment of others. Forgiving oneself and moving forward to awaiting opportunities makes for a spiritually healthy person.

My father created a prayer, which he added to the traditional grace said at mealtime. It has become a legend in our extended families. Reciting the simple words reminds us of the importance of sharing our time, talents, and treasure with others. In an effort to foster self-forgiveness, perhaps we could tweak it just a bit by adding two words: "Lord, *forgive us*, and help us to be mindful of the needs of others." As we pray, so we shall live.

I imagine a person who has learned to forgive oneself as well as others to be like the contented fly fisherman I observed in eastern Canada. Dressed in vest, cap, waders, and long-sleeved shirt, he confidently stood waist deep in water. With pipe in mouth and rhythmic twist of the wrist, he cast the willowy yellow line, then strategically pulled it toward him in hopes that the "big one" might snag itself on the fly hook. As he patiently used creative skill and wit, he absorbed the quiet solitude and peace, forgiving himself – like the adult parent – for each missed opportunity to be a better fisherman.

Is there an incident or segment in your life that requires self-forgiveness?

What strategies help you to forgive yourself?

I Must Be About God's Business

The world at large harbors sisters and brothers with special physical, emotional, spiritual, and mental needs. Thus, volunteers from every race, creed, age, gender, ethnicity, and skill-ability are needed to do His work. There is a vast amount of labor to be completed, each moment of every day not to be wasted away in idleness.

Now that spouse and grown children care ably for themselves, I feel called to continue my journey of doing God's business. Hence, the writing of these short stories, publishing a book, and offering the proceeds to charity.

The opportunities for being about God's business are endless: assisting hospitals and nursing homes; teaching immigrants; and volunteering at a church, synagogue, mosque, school, or civic organization. In analyzing the community needs as well as our own talents, we are able to discern the appropriate path of service to others.

As authentically kind and compassionate people, we can proceed on our daily travels, assisting those who are open to our care. With each person of integrity making a difference, our community, nation, and world *can* become an enormous circle of human beings, like diverse children holding hands in preparation for a ring-around-the rosy game.

Imagine the world peace, justice, and prosperity experienced when this scenario occurs. Awesome! It *can* happen – yet it must begin within our hearts, followed by the manner in which we treat others, and a willing spirit to help create a more benevolent society. As a human race, we can advance toward our mission of helping others in ways and in places that utilize our unique talents and gifts, fostering peaceful cohabitation on our planet.

How are you going about God's business?

What changes do you wish to make to your current life plan?

I Remember

W hile visiting my parents on their ranch, I remember the most beautiful sunset near the Dakota Badlands. As the sun gradually eased out of sight, pink, red, violet, and light blue hues spread across the broad horizon. Perhaps the quiet solitude also made the moment and view majestic, heavenly, and serene. Only God, in His supreme glory, could have created this evening of magnificent sunset and peaceful serenity.

A favorite elementary school principal, Ms. Jones, introduced me to mini-sabbaticals. She said, "Take five minutes to walk around the school building and surrounding block." She continued, "The fresh air and exercise will invigorate your body and spirit for dealing with the day's developing issues." Always, I will be grateful to this wise woman for her sound advice, as my school counselor responsibilities could, at times, be notoriously challenging, intense, and stressful. Child abuse and suicide threats comprised the most physically and emotionally draining of all issues.

How does one capture energizing pauses for spiritual rejuvenation? How does a person carry the calmness of serene moments throughout the day, into the night, and following week? In practicing contemplative arts, taking daily mini-sabbaticals, or absorbing nature's beauty, one can capture this peace and harbor it within the spirit, like a child who has discovered a treasured seashell while playing on a sandy beach. It is this peace that helps create a balanced spirit, a kind demeanor, and a close union with the Creator.

Whenever possible take a few moments to capture the consoling gift of a sunset. In a small corner of the brain, tuck away a mental picture of the tranquil beauty to be remembered on some intense or dreary day.

Describe a serene setting you have experienced.

What are your strategies for physical and spiritual rejuvenation, and in dealing with the demands of your lifestyle?

ℒife as a ℛose

W ith frost on the ground, a chill in the air, and Mother Earth ablaze in red, yellow, orange, purple, and green, I embarked upon an autumn vacation to a lovely Canadian setting. The colors seemed especially noteworthy when viewed along a nearby gentle river feeding into the quiet bay that led to the mighty sea. Yet, with all the fall beauty, the few final roses of summer, still blooming in front of the cottage, stimulated thoughts about the life-journey.

Although a bit of guilt surfaced when removing some of the beauty that others' behold, I cut one lone peace rose with three buds still hoping to bloom, and placed it in a slim marine blue vase. Several days of significant visual change transformed the cutting into an almost petal-less stem, except for the tightly closed buds. This living and dying transformation took place before my eyes, with only one constant: the same sweet perfume, the very essence of this unique rose.

The bud, the womb of the rose, tightly protects the potential beauty of each flower. Nourished through the stem, it prepares for its "birth," gradually exhibiting its beauty to the world, as in the birthing process of a precious human being. Like the never-to-be-opened bud, some unborn children don't graduate to the birthing process, or do so scathed in some way, unable to survive. Yet their very beings, their presence, are remembered forever.

The partially opened bud, or a human being whose development is hindered by physical or mental delays, is especially unique as it struggles to absorb nutrients from the stem for strength to remain erect. The process appears similar to that of a developmentally delayed adult; a person who chooses to be stagnant in life's learning process; or the world's repressed women, children, and men who are ill-treated, undernourished, or plagued with illness. They, too, are special buds who will not bloom into full potential as intended by the Creator.

The life of the fully opened blossom, cut off in mid-bloom, becomes shortened, like a thirty-something person who dies while still unfolding, developing, and honing special talents and character. Nevertheless, each petal gradually displayed itself, delicately framing and protecting the center petals, like one's inner spirit and self-esteem. Within a few days, the rose reached its mature beauty. Then gradually, one by one, petals fell on to the kitchen table.

During the rose's last stage of life, the petals fell in a creative design around the vase with one lone petal resting on a leaf, not quite ready to make the final drop. Similarly, as people experience life, they gather wisdom, one of the precious gifts of aging. They learn to listen more, speak less, and to squeeze out the positive gifts of each day. Like the falling petals, they have lessons and stories to offer while sharing inner beauty with those who take time to be present to them. Community volunteers, family, and friends of those in the "dropping-petals" stage gain much inspiration from elders. In so doing, they offer gifts of the nourishment of time, as well as physical and spiritual assistance to maturing adults.

The final remains of the rose petals, now fallen from the stem, may be dried for potpourri and strewn on a rose bed or buried with a special marker, similar to the ashes of loved ones. Choices. Always choices. But the delicate sweet fragrance, in itself a gift, like a person's spirit within, lingers on, to be cradled by grieving hearts.

I remember the thrill of a red rose presented to me in Okinawa; a dozen long-stemmed red roses brought on the airplane from Washington, D.C.; a ceramic rose-decorated dinner bell presented in South Carolina. Likewise, I recall red roses arranged with white baby's breath delivered with brotherly love; lavender roses gracing the arm of a dinner guest; wild roses cut and hidden behind my smiling father's back, then presented to my mother.

The beauty of roses abounds worldwide, always with the same delicate perfume. It matters not that they are hybrids or common variety, wild or nursery grown, soft or brilliantly colored. Roses are like people, for they each bring interesting variety and beauty to the world, creating artistic majesty whether alone or viewed in a precisely arranged bouquet.

This morning, I placed a fresh new rose in the marine blue vase, offering joy and hope, like that of a newborn baby initiating smiles and whispers of gratitude to new parents. All according to design, the cycle of life continues around the globe.

Describe a rose, or any special flower, that has meaning to you.
How have flowers graced and enhanced your life?

Okay, Let's Do It

Adult children can be such a kick at times. Catalysts for change – patience – forgiving. One intriguing event illustrates a son's effort to inspire his mother toward a healthier-you goal.

Early one morning, my son called from a faraway city and said, "Mom, next May I'm coming for a visit. How about if we spend a day at the spa together?"

"Well...uh...sure," I stuttered. "That sounds like a great idea!" I must admit, however, that his proposal caught me off-guard.

"Oh," he continued. "And how about if you check out different ones in the area, select a facility, and together we'll make it happen?"

Again, I found myself slowly replying, "Well...uh...sure."

I know nothing about spas. Fitness walking is familiar territory, but my life-experience never included stepping one foot into any type of build-a-better-you facility!

As a dutiful mother, though, I proceeded to search the yellow pages, make phone calls, and ask friends for references. Hearing the description of one location fostered a maybe-this-is-the-right-one reaction.

May arrived, as did son from faraway city. Being open to new experiences, we traveled to a mountain retreat for a day of physical and spiritual renewal. After a spectacular drive through a canyon that frames a rapidly moving stream, we left the main highway, proceeding on a minimally maintained road. Several rustic buildings, nestled in the forest, came into view, one of which claimed the "Office" sign. With car parked, we turned to each other and sighed. Then, he said, "Okay, let's do it!"

Inching forward, as if walking into a building for an initial interview, we relaxed when greeted by a gracious resident yogi dressed in simple blouse and long, flowered skirt.

"Welcome," she said softly. "Let's review your day. The first half-hour will be spent in breath awareness (prana) followed by an hour of classical hatha yoga. After one half-hour meditation to quiet the mind and discover the Inner Self, you are invited to have a vegetarian lunch with other yogis and guests. In the afternoon, you each are scheduled for an hour of full-body massage to further help relax the body and mind."

We looked at one another, and this time I cheerily said, "Okay, let's do it."

I could only imagine what was going through this athletic son's head as I stretch to bend, balance, and follow the agile instructor's yoga directions. I almost fell once with my not-so-agile body bent at the waist, eyes focused directly ahead, arms stretched to the side in a bird-like form, and balancing on one leg. Yet never a smirk or rolling of son's eyes did I see! So very kind and patient of him to accept my clumsiness.

Prepared with homegrown ingredients, the healthy vegetarian lunch satisfied our hearty appetites. An afternoon walk amongst the aspen groves, patches of remaining winter snow, and lush meadows nurtured our physical beings. While savoring the rhythmic sounds of the spring-filled streams, I breathed in fresh mountain air which composed the spirit within.

After this bit of exercise in nature's natural spa, we prepared ourselves for the massage. The therapists used hands, oils, and lotions, as they silently repeated mantras to release tensions. At the end of the session, the body, mind, and spirit truly felt rejuvenated, refreshed, renewed, and healed. Leaving the private room, I felt injected with a liter of self-confidence, and whispered to myself, *"Wow, I'm ready to face the world again!"*

Driving home after this day spent at a residential ashram, I turned to my son and asked, "What did you think of this new experience?"

"Well," he replied, "it wasn't exactly what I had in mind. But I enjoyed it."

"And, just exactly what *did* you have in mind for this day?" I queried.

"Uh…well," he stammered, "I envisioned a day of swimming, weight-lifting, cycling. Maybe even having you spend time with a personal trainer."

"Oh," I muttered.

"But," he concluded, "we spent time together, experienced a new spa setting and treatment program. It *was* a great day. And I look forward to the next 'Okay, let's do it!' adventure."

"Yes," I agreed, grateful for having taken time to rest and recharge in a peaceful mountain setting.

Secretly, I promised myself that in the future, before scheduling a day's activities with faraway son, I would ask a few questions. On the other hand, if I glean more particulars, I might not escape all that weight-lifting and personal training hoopla.

Recall an activity that turned out a bit different than you had envisioned.

What were the "hits and misses" of the experience?

Please Pass the Butter

At one of my college reunions, a former alumna and I had a brief discussion about family members who no longer practice the same religion as we do. I shared that when I visit my children, I attend *their* religious service, whether or not it is of a different orientation. With a shocked look, yet trying to be tactful, she firmly stated, "According to our catechism, those who participate in other religious services commit sin." I equally was shocked that someone, so many years after significant church changes, could harbor such a belief.

Yes, I believe in being an active member of the oldest church in history. I accept its traditions and faults, similar to remaining a part of an imperfect country, state, workplace, or family. On the other hand, I also am open to the spiritual beliefs of others, respectful of their choices in creating their own earthly paths, and aware that they, too, are responsible for their actions.

My immediate and extended family members are kind, generous, and loving people who strive to serve others. I cannot imagine a loving Creator not opening His arms to them as well as to other people who incorporate various spiritual practices into their lives. To support this belief, a person need only review the lesson of *acceptance of others* dramatically illustrated in the biblical woman-caught-in-adultery story wherein Jesus challenges her accusers to "throw the first stone."

So, then, how do we care for ourselves as we meet with other people, and sometimes discuss confrontational issues? Oftentimes, it helps to:

- Keep in mind the importance of maintaining our own balance and calm while respecting the beliefs and values of others.

- Acknowledge the other person's right to personal opinions, then state that it is equally accepting to express our own.
- Proceed to share personal ideas and beliefs, if the situation feels open to an intelligent discussion. Otherwise, change the subject or excuse oneself from the situation.

Conflicting opinions in the world of work may require different strategies, which are many and varied.

My father, a quiet-mannered gentleman, lived by the motto, "If you can't say something nice about someone, don't say anything at all." Naturally, his encouragement to follow the same behavioral pattern became instilled in his children at an early age. My father learned his gentle, patient ways from his mother Aleah, as his father tended to be domineering in stature, manner, and voice.

The motto traveled with him as he served in the United States Navy during World War I, experienced life as a shepherd in the Dakotas, and in his fifty-eight years as a merchant managing a general store. He was regarded highly by Native Americans who respected him as a generous, honest, and kind gentleman.

Another life-long guide that served him well was, "Keep your sense of humor, or life will get the best of you." Cutting out humorous cartoons and funny stories, he shared them with others when they needed a "picker-upper."

Although well-mannered, his Irish orneriness surfaced when passing the butter dish at the dining table. If one weren't cautious, a thumb ended up in the butter as he passed the dish. Or, he would toss it across the table to the person requesting the condiment. My mother, the Chief Operating Officer, made it clear early on that if a dish were ever broken, she would buy a new set of dishes. Guess what? Nary a chip occurred during years of Dad and the seven children tossing the butter plate to one another. Actually, I think we all enjoyed the guests' shocked expressions as we put on a show for them!

Religion, as well as politics, can be potentially volatile subjects. Yet each can be discussed within the realm of equal respect for the other person's values, beliefs, and opinions. Likewise, analyzing the positive lessons learned from communicative experiences provides valuable personal growth for future encounters. My experience has shown that – like using crutches while a broken leg heals – engaging a sense of humor as well as conflict management strategies often support people in working through stressful situations and conflicting discussions.

Describe a conflict situation with which you are challenged?

What do you find working for you? What changes need to be made?

Rekindling the Spirit Within

W alking exercises the body, refreshes the mind, and generates creative thoughts, but it also can provide opportunities to rekindle the Spirit within. In listening to one of many audiobooks, I learned that famous writers like G. K. Chesterton, Charles Dickinson, and C. S. Lewis were walkers. I am not familiar with the exercise habits of persons from other artistic venues. My best guess is that they, too, discover energy-producing exercises that fill their creativity cup.

The setting for rekindling-walks is paramount. Such nurturing scenes I have been blessed to experience on the Switzerland forest pathways, Monterey Peninsula boardwalks, Colorado mountain trails, New Zealand countryside, and various city parks. But never have I felt the depth of the rekindled fire as I did on a recent trip to Canada.

On the northeastern side of Nova Scotia is a town settled hundreds of years ago by the French who, escaping persecution from the English, created this area's Acadian settlement. From this location, people can drive to a small, sparsely inhabited island, which is ideal for inspirational walks. Parking near the weathered wharf, I set afoot along the grassy coastline, like a laborer escaping the fatigue of daily toils, searching for my spiritual lighthouse's beacon of light. Not another person or animal was visible, except for a fuzzy brown and black caterpillar inching its way along the path, and bees buzzing around the dwarfed conifer trees – a perfect setting for contemplating God's Spirit within, that unique presence and glow surrounded by human flesh and bones.

As I climbed in solitude with a strong wind to the back, my heart rate began to accelerate and the endorphins release, both of which stimulate mental alertness and creativity. Viewed from fifty feet above, the angry waves seemed to be in an Olympic race to reach the shoreline, crashing against the rocky cliffs. I pondered, *How could anyone be desperate enough to cast themselves off such a steep incline to the unforgiving boulders below?*

Nearby was an old wooden sign with the weathered message, "Grave Site." Inscriptions on three flat stone markings disappeared long ago from the harsh winds and wet storms. One lone upright marker appeared to have been totally destroyed, for only the base remained. A few words, "Mother" and "Beloved Son," could be deciphered. Recording of the date had sunk below ground. I surmised that this desolate site protected remains of early eighteenth century inhabitants, settlers searching for their own freedom, inspiration, and spiritual lighthouse.

Indeed, this free-spirited, coastal setting rekindled God's presence within me, like a blazing, freshly lighted bonfire. Here, on this serene coastal island, my desire and commitment to continue with service to other inhabitants of Mother Earth became clearly defined and energized.

Describe a memorable experience that rekindled your spirit.

Where do your desires and commitments become renewed and energized?

The Agony of Loss

How can anyone adequately express comforting words to help suture hurting hearts and assist with the painful healing process? Without a doubt, losing a loved one, especially one's own child, is an excruciating period of sorrow and challenge.

When faced with a traumatic event, one may wonder, *How will I ever get through this terrible time?* In reality, people do not get *over* the loss of a treasured loved one; but with God's help and that of relatives and friends, they manage to get *through* it. The passing of time, support from understanding resources, and prayers assist in easing the pain. Sometimes, too, it helps to remember the adage, *Life is not a test. It's okay to ask for help.* Emotionally injured individuals may be able to accept encouragement, support, and comfort from empathetic others as they help carry the heavy burden of loss.

Truly, children are God's most precious blessings to a couple. Yet they are, indeed, just that – blessings. These gifts are to be loved, nurtured, and enjoyed for as long as He wills. Once a child's death occurs, memories of moments together become more precious than ever and aid in soothing broken hearts. Parents may ask, "Why? Why did our child die?" I don't believe we ever find answers to these types of questions on this earth. Years after the stillborn death of my firstborn son, I concluded, as a strategy for easing the sorrow, that he entered eternity first so that he could watch over the rest of his family and guide us on our journeys.

Another person cannot feel the deep pain that stabs at the hearts of those dealing with a significant loss, nor the many peaks and valleys experienced as they work through the grieving stages. But, as far-fetched as it may sound, in time, emotionally injured people may find themselves healed to the point wherein they can reach out to help someone else who is working through a significant loss. I judge that this is all a part of the living-dying-caring cycle.

Grieving also is not age-specific. A child misplacing a favorite toy, giving up a familiar sleeping area like a crib, or losing a tooth may ignite feelings of sadness and anger. Likewise, changing schools, moving to another location, divorce, or new blended families may be a source of sadness to young children. According to grief counselors, the stages of shock, depression, anger, bargaining, and acceptance are all normal parts of the grieving process. Change will stimulate these stages, setting the healing process into motion, similar to shifting an automatic car into the "drive" position.

Dealing with grief is different at various stages of our lives. Several personal scenarios come to mind. One day my father approached me after I returned home from a day at school. With as much understanding as he could muster up, he said, "I'm sorry, Meg, but your dog was run over by a car today." A few years later, I remember feeling a terrible homesickness after leaving home at age thirteen to attend boarding school. Leaving the United States to live in a foreign country with spouse and three small children presented a huge loss in not being able to see my parents, family members, friends, and colleagues for three years. Then, when the youngest child left for college, the empty nest monster asserted itself, presenting me with a lonely heart.

Presently living with a hearing-challenged person makes for more quiet solitude. My mother used to say, "God allows our eyesight to worsen as we mature so that we don't notice the dust as much." Perhaps He also allows hearing loss so that we will be comfortable with silence as well as create more time for quiet contemplation.

Sorrowing people feel pain. Gradually the spirit heals. While life is forever changed after any type of loss, at some point grieving individuals do feel some sense of peace, hope, and joy once again.

Tell about a significant loss in your lifetime.

What strategies did you find useful in working through the challenging period?

The Great Spirit

"How has God, the Great Spirit, worked in your life and history?" asked the seminar facilitator, a Native American of the Lakota tribe. Unable to pen a response within the allotted time, I chose to think through a somewhat realistic overview before committing it to paper. After days of pondering this question as I exercised, drove the car, and scrubbed bathrooms, a clear synopsis became focused in my mind. Sometimes, it just takes periods of silence and thought process for conclusions to be drawn.

As the Lakota facilitator continued to relay the history of Nicholas Black Elk, I remembered my acquaintance with his son. Ben worked at South Dakota's Mount Rushmore for years, accommodating tourists requesting to be photographed with him in his native costume. As the leader continued her story, based on facts from *Black Elk Speaks*, she noted that the great Lakota leader was buried in the same cemetery as my maternal grandparents. At that point, I began to consider how my life intertwined with the Native Americans; how their spiritual beliefs significantly influenced my life, especially their devotion to Mother Earth and the Spirit World.

For me, the influence of the Great Spirit, and the humble, honest Native Americans whose paths crossed mine, seemed to parallel the influence of my kind, compassionate, and humble father. He harbored a great respect for the tribal elders, perhaps unknowingly identifying with the similarity in their personal characteristics and spiritual beliefs.

The Notre Dame Sisters, who lived nearby and schooled the O'Neill children until high school began, fondly remember my father carrying a full sack of groceries each week. Faithfully, he drew a caricature of a little man wearing an alpine hat on the brown bag. Presenting the gift to the Sisters after Sunday service, he teasingly said, "Someone left this on our doorstep with a note stating specific instructions to give it to you."

Many times, as Native Americans requested assistance, my father either wrote notes that could be used for credit in the local store, or gave cash for their immediate needs. Later in life, as I visited my parents, I once offered gratuity to a Lakota gentleman who helped with their yardwork. Not to be outdone, the next day he knocked at our door and presented me with earrings made from pieces of porcupine quills encircled with red and white beads. Kind acts, it seems, have a way of continually moving forward, like restless tumble-weeds rolling toward the Nebraska Sand Hills.

One summer, when I was about eleven or twelve years old, I recall assisting Oglala Lakota women with drying yellow corn for the local community school. We placed many ears of corn on a large screen and left them to dry for several days. We then rubbed the corncobs on the screen until the kernels fell off. Once removed, we collected the dried corn and placed it in jars for future stews and soups. Similarly, I observed my own mother, maternal grandmother, and neighboring women sitting around a large quilt frame making tiny stitches on future heirlooms or raffle items. The two work scenarios contained one common goal: to benefit the community.

Living on a reservation enhanced my life by being educated with the Native Americans through the first eight grades, and by our working together in my parents' store. Sun Dances with natives clad in beaded dress and dancing to rhythmic beats of the drums, and their life-celebration-funeral rites left vivid impressions of their devotion to the Great Spirit.

After death occurs, I envision spirits passing through a purple clematis-adorned archway into eternity. Do I feel spirits nearby sometimes? Do I call upon them to assist us as in the Native American tradition? Sometimes, yes. I sense the spirit of my mother, grandmother, and sister-in-law in beautiful garden areas, for they toiled the earth and loved the resulting beauty. I sense my father when I visit the ocean and Mission areas, for he served in the United States Navy, enjoyed California beaches, and assisted monetarily with the work of numerous missionaries. Finally, the spirit of my first-born son is felt around the world as he carries out his mother's request to protect his brothers, their spouses, and families as they travel their own journeys.

While Nicholas Black Elk turned to the Morning Star each day for wisdom, I am nourished by the sun's energy and the moon's calm vibes of hope, support, and evening peace. Being near water tends to be inspiring as well. Earthen colors portrayed in the four seasons offer a palette of beauty; her animals, fish, and birds bring pleasure and nutrition; fresh air cleanses and provides freshness to the lungs. In the spirit of preservation, Mother Earth and the entire universe are to be enjoyed, respected, used, and kept sacred for future generations.

The Great Spirit, the Master Designer and Engineer of the Universe, our Guide and Protector, Allah, God, Yahweh. Whatever a person believes the Higher Power to be, the words of Nicholas Black Elk ring true for all spiritual beliefs. He stated that all things are the work of the Great Spirit. Without a doubt, I am grateful to the Native Americans who taught me respect and love for life, the universe, the Spirit World, and the Divine Creator of all.

What childhood experiences influenced your current spiritual beliefs?
How do your current spiritual beliefs differ from that of your childhood?

The Umbrella

Where is it? I know it's somewhere in this bag with polartec gloves and hats, earmuffs, and handwarmers! Scrounging through extra items kept in the car trunk seemed a necessity, given the numerous days and nights of June rain. After dry, hot weather of past years, it was rather an anomaly to be searching desperately, almost in a panic mode, for an umbrella. Once located, I struggled with opening it, as it had been years since its use in this drought-plagued state. Forgetting how it operated, I struggled to get it taut. Imagine such a scene on this summer solstice, with torrents of rain, fifty degree temperatures, and snowfall forcing road closures in the Rocky Mountains just eighty miles west of the mile-high city!

Once walking with umbrella in hand, though, I felt a presence of peace and hope: *peace* with the overhead umbrella allowing my clothes to remain dry; *hope* with the welcome moisture bringing life to thirsty grass, shrubs, trees, flowers, and crops. The experience reminded me that both peace and hope accompany most events in life: like the peaceful death of a sick, elderly relative, and the hope that this person is no longer in pain; the peace following an energetic discussion where one is able to express thoughts and feelings, and the hope that positive change will come from the verbal exchange. The peace experienced after positive conferences with children's teachers; the hope that is extended for their continuing on the path of success. The peace felt after an ill friend survives surgery; the hope that the convalescent period will be successful. The peace felt after an invigorating jog or walk; the hope that the exercise strategy will make for a healthier life. The peace felt when offered a career position after a lengthy search for the right job; the hope that all works out well with the change. The peace that comes from working through the grieving process after the loss of a loved one; the hope that one will never hurt that way again.

Interestingly, the buried umbrella fostered *peace* and *hope* on this summer day, while stimulating racing thoughts and metaphors about life moments. It behooves us to listen to the messages from the heart, and, with gratitude, look for the gifts buried deep within our daily experiences.

Select a "tool" you found useful today. What might it symbolize?

Where can you find gifts of peace and hope in a recent experience?

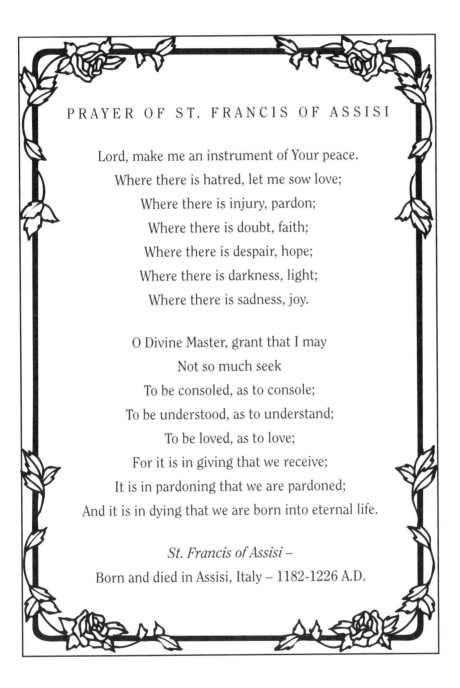

PRAYER OF ST. FRANCIS OF ASSISI

Lord, make me an instrument of Your peace.
Where there is hatred, let me sow love;
Where there is injury, pardon;
Where there is doubt, faith;
Where there is despair, hope;
Where there is darkness, light;
Where there is sadness, joy.

O Divine Master, grant that I may
Not so much seek
To be consoled, as to console;
To be understood, as to understand;
To be loved, as to love;
For it is in giving that we receive;
It is in pardoning that we are pardoned;
And it is in dying that we are born into eternal life.

St. Francis of Assisi –
Born and died in Assisi, Italy – 1182-1226 A.D.

INSPIRING RESOURCES

Albom, Mitch. *The Five People You Will Meet in Heaven*. New York: Hyperion, 2003.

Albom, Mitch. *Tuesdays with Morrie*. New York: Doubleday, 1997.

Angelo, Maya. *All God's Children Need Traveling Shoes*. New York: Random House, 1997.

Benson, Herbert, M.D. *Timeless Healing*. New York: Fireside, 1996.

Black, Cynthia. *Our Turn, Our Time*. Oregon: Beyond Words Publishing, 2000.

Breathnach, Sarah Ban. *Simple Abundance*. New York: Warner Books, 1995.

Brokaw, Tom. *The Greatest Generation*. New York: Random House, 1998.

Callanan, Maggie & Kelley, Patricia. *Final Gifts*. New York: Bantam, 1997.

Cameron, Julia & Goldberg, Natalie. *The Writing Life*. Colorado: Sounds True, 1999.

Dillard, Annie. *An American Childhood*. New York: Harper and Row, 1987.

Frankl, Viktor. *Man's Search for Meaning*. Boston: Beacon Press, 1992.

Goldberg, Natalie. *Writing Down the Bones*. Boston: Shambhala, 1998.

Gonzalez-Balado, Jose Luis. *Mother Teresa in Her Own Words*. New York: Random House, 1996.

Goodall, Jane. *A Reason for Hope: A Spiritual Journey*. New York: Warner Books, 1999.

Guthrie, Elizabeth, M.D., & Matthews, Kathy. *The Trouble with Perfect*. New York: Broadway Books, 2002.

Hay, Louise L. *You Can Heal Your Life*. California: Hay House Inc., 1999.

Karr, Katherine. *Taking Time for Me: How Caregivers Can Effectively Deal with Stress*. New York: Prometheus Books, 1992.

Keith, Kent M. *Anyway*. New York: The Berkley Publishing Group, 2004.

Kidd, Sue Monk. *The Secret Life of Bees*. New York: Penguin Books, 2003.

Klauser, Henriette Anne. *Write It Down, Make It Happen.* New York: Simon and Schuster, 2001.

Lambert, Mary. *Clearing the Clutter for Good Feng Shui.* London: Cima Books Ltd., 2001.

Lozoff, Bo. *It's a Meaningful Life.* New York: Viking Arkana, 2000.

McBride, James. *The Color of Water.* New York: Riverhead Books, 1996.

Miller, Patti. *Writing Your Life.* Australia: Allen & Unwin, 2001.

Mitchell, W. *Taking Responsibility for Your Choices.* Colorado: Career Track Publications, 1996.

Neihardt, John G. *Black Elk Speaks.* Nebraska: University of Nebraska Press, 2000.

Norris, Kathleen. *Dakota: A Spiritual Geography.* Boston: Houghton Mifflin, 2001.

Norris, Kathleen. *The Cloistered Walk.* New York: The Berkley Publishing Group, 1996.

Rather, Dan. *The American Dream: Stories from the Heart of Our Nation.* New York: William Morrow, 2001.

Reeve, Christopher. *Still Me.* New York: Random House, 1998.

Richardson, Jan L. *Sacred Journeys.* Tennessee: Upper Room Books, 1995.

Roberts, Cokie. *We Are Our Mothers' Daughters.* New York: William Morrow & Company, Inc., 1998.

Ryan, M. J. *Attitudes of Gratitude.* California: Conari Press, 1999.

Schachter-Shalomi, Zalman & Miller, Ronald S. *From Age-ing to Sage-ing.* New York: Warner Books, 1997.

Siegel, Bernie S., M.D. *Humor and Healing.* Colorado: Sounds True, 1990.

Siegel, Bernie S., M.D. *365 Prescriptions for the Soul.* California: New World Library, 2004.

St. James, Elaine. *Living the Simple Life.* New York: Hyperion, 1996.

Svoboda, Melannie. *Traits of a Healthy Spirituality*. Connecticut: Twenty-Third Publications, 1998.

Tamaro, Susanna. *Follow Your Heart*. New York: Talese/Doubleday, 1995.

Tsering, Diki. *Dalai Lama, My Son*. New York: Viking Arkans, 2000.

Vardey, Lucinda. *Mother Teresa: A Simple Path*. New York: Ballantine Books, 1995.

Waitley, Denis. *The New Dynamics of Winning*. New York: William Morrow, 1993.

Warren, Rick. *The Purpose Driven Life*. Michigan: Zondervan, 2002.

Wilkenson, Bruce. *The Prayer of Jabez*. Oregon: Multnomah, 2000.

Will, George F. *The Pursuit of Happiness and Other Sobering Thoughts*. Audio Cassette, Maryland: Prince Frederick, 1986.

Willard, Tom. *Wings of Honor*. New York: Forge, 1999.

Notes